Preparing for Student Teaching in a Pluralistic Classroom

Preparing for Student Teaching in a Pluralistic Classroom

Timothy R. Blair
University of Central Florida

Deneese L. Jones
University of Kentucky

Allyn and Bacon

Boston ♦ London ♦ Toronto ♦ Sydney ♦ Tokyo ♦ Singapore

Senior Editor: Virginia Lanigan
Editorial Assistant: Kris Lamarre
Senior Marketing Manager: Kathy Hunter
Editorial–Production Administrator: Donna Simons
Editorial–Production Service: Shepherd, Inc.
Composition and Prepress Buyer: Linda Cox
Manufacturing Buyer: Suzanne Lareau
Cover Administrator: Jenny Hart

Library of Congress Cataloging-in-Publication Data

Blair, Timothy R.
    Preparing for student teaching in a pluralistic classroom / by
Timothy R. Blair and Deneese L. Jones.
        p.   cm.
    Includes bibliographical references and index.
    ISBN 0-205-26761-0 (alk. paper)
    1. Student teaching—United States. 2. Pluralism (Social
sciences)—United States. 3. Teachers—Self-rating of—United
States. I. Jones, Deneese L. (Deneese LaKay), 1952-
II. Title
    LB2157.U5B57   1998
    370'.71'0973—dc21   97-28839
                                                        CIP

Printed in the United States of America
10 9 8 7 6 5 4 3 2   02 01 00 99 98

Contents

Preface

Audience

This text is intended for teacher education students completing their student teaching experiences and other future teachers observing and teaching in elementary and secondary classrooms. The content of the text and its reflective activities are designed to be partially self-instructional in nature and may serve as discussion topics for student teaching seminars, small-group coaching meetings, and professional education classes.

Purpose

Considerable attention has been directed to meeting the needs of diverse populations in our schools. It is becoming widely recognized that schools need to restructure their efforts in accepting and effectively teaching students from different cultural and linguistic backgrounds. Today, more than ever before, classrooms represent multiracial, multicultural, and multiethnic backgrounds. Many classrooms have students representing more than a dozen languages and many ethnic and racial backgrounds. This enormous cultural diversity and greater variety of backgrounds offer exciting challenges and responsibilities for teachers.

The purpose of this book is fourfold: first, to prepare teacher education students for teaching in a culturally pluralistic society; second, to cover the essential information on the components of the student teaching experience; third, to provide future teachers with the content and strategies of effective teaching methods for all students; and fourth, to help future teachers develop a questioning, self-monitoring, and reflective attitude toward their own decision-making in teaching.

Interwoven with the elements of successful student teaching, this book will also help foster both sensitivity and effective teaching decisions for all children depending upon cultural and linguistic backgrounds. Principles of effective instruction for all students will be described and numerous practical examples will be provided that illustrate how they may be implemented in the classroom. Each chapter will provide at least one reflective assignment to implement important concepts and/or teaching strategies discussed. Many of the assignments require structured observation and feedback. Also, instructors and professors are encouraged to have students work cooperatively in collecting data and analyzing teaching techniques. These assignments serve as self-monitoring devices to help teachers-in-preparation become more conscious of effective instructional practices. The authors agree wholeheartedly with the many teacher educators who are calling for an increased emphasis in preservice programs on students participating and interacting vis-à-vis the teaching process with their peers and with public school and university personnel. David Berliner has called for meaningful opportunities for future teachers to discuss, practice, integrate, and learn various aspects of the teaching role with other professionals in a more laboratory-based setting (*Journal of Teacher Education,* Nov.–Dec. 1985; Research Symposium Address at ATE Annual Conference, 1987). For students to become analytical of their attitude toward teaching, they need to have experiences that sharpen their observation skills along with opportunities to discuss these findings with their peers and interested professionals. B.O. Smith, in *A Design for a School of Pedagogy* (Washington, D.C.: U.S. Government Printing Office, 1980), accentuates the importance of observation. Speaking to domains of training in becoming a teacher, Smith noted: "The first domain, the one that permeates all the others, is observation. The ability to observe a phenomenon objectively is one of the primary marks of a professional in any field . . . . For a teacher who cannot tell what is going on will be unable to respond appropriately and effectively to the events" (p. 84).

It is the authors' contention that teachers in preparation should be provided teaching principles that reflect culturally responsive pedagogy. Furthermore, they should have opportunities to practice these teaching principles in diverse classroom settings. A practical time to examine and practice effective teaching strategies is during the various "field experiences" designed for teacher education candidates. This time may be during student teaching, during an internship in the schools, or in a multitude of other clinical or early field experiences. These contacts with students in actual classroom situations, whether brief or extended, serve a variety of purposes including learning the teaching role and gaining an understanding of learning, of students, and of the nature of schools themselves.

Although field experiences generally receive good grades from teacher education graduates, skepticism exists regarding the effectiveness of such experiences, largely due to a lack of conceptual framework or research base. The common thread in field experience programs should be those teaching principles derived from both research and expert opinion that promote culturally responsive instruction.

It is the sincere wish of the authors that readers utilize the information presented in this book to become increasingly cognizant of what they are doing or not doing; what needs to be improved; what needs to be modified, expanded, or omitted; what factors impede teaching; and how students react to what the teacher is doing. Those preparing to teach should learn where to put their time and effort. They also need to be challenged to be reflective, self-monitoring educators, capable of further growth and development. All students need and deserve such quality teachers, and it is the aim of this book to help produce them.

We'd like to thank the following reviewers for their valuable comments and suggestions: Mary Bay, University of Illinois at Chicago; Linda Brookhart, University of Northern Colorado; Dr. Kathleen E. Fite, Southwest Texas State University; Kathryn L. Liptak, Wesley College; Robert Press, Governors State University; Nancy Reese, Baylor University; Alexander Sapiens, San Jose State University; and Joan Shiring, University of Texas—Austin.

A Message to Teachers-in-Preparation

Importance of Being a Self-Monitor

As a teacher-in-preparation, you are eager for reliable information on how you can be an effective teacher. The purpose of this text is to further your progress in becoming a professional teacher. Today classrooms are full of diverse learners and you must be prepared and feel confident in interacting with all students in your classroom. In addition to specifically discussing how to be successful in your student teaching experience, principles of culturally responsive instruction will be presented and discussed in various chapters. You will be encouraged to apply and reflect on each principle of instruction in your own subject(s) and classroom. After a succinct discussion of each principle of instruction, many practical suggestions will be given to help you improve your teaching. Unfortunately, no simple formula can be given for all classrooms. A formula for effective instruction for all students, regardless of race/ethnicity, gender, socioeconomic status, language, age, grade, interests, needs, learning styles, and learning rate is incompatible with our knowledge of students and learning. What is compatible with it, however, is the development of a self-monitoring, reflective attitude that generates useful information about the students, the content being taught, the classroom context and physical environment, and possible teaching strategies to accomplish your goals.

This text is based on the following proposition: Teachers who engage in a process of monitoring their own teaching become more confident in their abilities and are able to provide the instruction all students need. An approach to teaching based on this proposition encourages you to become a self-monitor. Self-monitors reflect about their teaching and ask, "Why am I doing what I am doing?" By becoming a self-monitor, you will be able to recognize student needs and determine the right course of action. Self-monitoring should be a continuous process that makes you cognizant of strengths and challenges in an instructional program and points the way for further diagnosis or modification of the existing program. The process of self-monitoring is facilitated by systematically observing classroom events and by having a friend or colleague observe and provide feedback on your teaching. Once you have collected information on your teaching, you are in a position to reflect on the information and discuss your perceptions with your college supervisors, cooperating teachers, and fellow teachers-in-preparation. Through this process of reflection, you will improve the

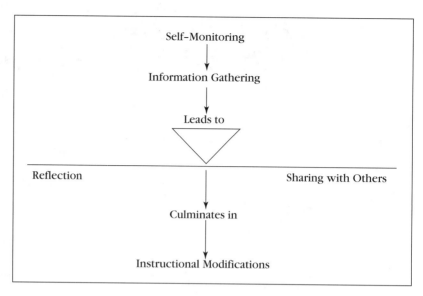

Self-Monitoring

Information Gathering

Leads to

Reflection   Sharing with Others

Culminates in

Instructional Modifications

FIGURE A-1

process of learning in your classroom and become more confident in your teaching abilities. This process of self-monitoring is depicted in Figure A-1.

Becoming a Self-Monitor

Each chapter will focus on elements of successful student teaching and, most important, explain how to be a self-monitor for the topic being discussed. This is accomplished in three ways:

1. *Pause and Reflect: Self-Monitoring Activity* segments offer in-text assignments.
2. *Self-Monitoring FYIs* contain a full spectrum of teaching tips, ideas, and useful information.
3. *Thinking Like a Teacher: Recap of Major Ideas* are summary statements of the key ideas of each chapter.

The chapters will provide in-text activities and reflective assignments to involve you and help you monitor your teaching; for instance, by interviewing a teacher or having another student teacher or your supervising teacher observe and record data on an aspect of your instruction. These in-text self-monitoring assignments are labeled *Pause and Reflect: Self-Monitoring Activity.*

A second way to help you implement a self-monitoring attitude is the inclusion of short, informational segments labeled *Self-Monitoring FYIs,* found in various chapters. Each FYI focuses on an important topic related to the content of the chapter. The FYIs will provide you with practical information and teaching tips, points to remember, and brief discussions and explanations. You are encouraged to reflect on the information as it relates to your own situation, to try the ideas in the classroom, and to discuss the information with others.

The third way you will be encouraged to be a self-monitor in relation to your teaching is to reflect on the brief listing of summary statements at the end of each chapter, labeled *Thinking Like a Teacher: Recap of Major Ideas*. You are encouraged to discuss these statements with other students and teachers.

There are numerous methods of implementing the various principles of instruction and it is hoped you will adapt them to your own style. Furthermore, there is no one "correct" method—there are many styles depending on the situation. For each principle of instruction, it is recommended you try it out in one or more classes and ask yourself, "How does it work? Why did it happen this way? How might it work better next time?" In this way, you will not only be learning the principles of instruction and adjusting them to your situation, but you will also be developing ways to monitor your teaching. The ability to observe yourself honestly, monitor your teaching, and modify your teaching is a hallmark of a true professional.

Preparing for Student Teaching in a Pluralistic Classroom

Part I

Planning for Success

Chapter ONE

Developing a Multicultural Perspective

Critical to the preparation of a perspective of education that is multicultural is an awareness of the enormous demographic changes in the United States. In 1982 nearly three of four young people (ages 0 to 17) in the United States were European American (Pallas, Natriello, & McDill, 1989), but by 2020 only one of two young people will be European American. In 1982 only one of ten young people was Hispanic, while it is estimated that this figure will change to one of four in 2020. Over this same period, the number of children living in poverty is expected to increase by 37 percent, from 14.7 million to 20 million. Schools will need to serve 3.4 million more children living in poverty in 2020 than they served in 1984 (Au, 1993). These trends make it clear that the schooling of students of diverse backgrounds can no longer be viewed as an issue to be addressed through special or remedial programs that target at-risk students in each school. Such an awareness, further, brings about an imperative for each preservice teacher to have a sophisticated understanding of the increasing racial, ethnic, cultural, and socioeconomic class diversity in the nation's schools and classrooms. This chapter is designed to introduce student teachers to the major issues and concepts for multicultural education. In addition, student teachers will participate in several activities of knowledge construction that seek to provoke a continual awareness and need for multiple perspectives in successful classroom instruction.

The Role of Education That Is Multicultural

> Carolyn is a young Irish-American kindergarten teacher who has been teaching for five years. The school at which she has taught has been a predominantly white, middle-class school in a quiet neighborhood in New England. However, because of recent redistricting, the school population now includes children from a housing project not far away. These children are almost exclusively poor and Black. Thus, Carolyn and the other teachers in the school are newly faced with a population of children with whom they are completely unfamiliar (Delpit, 1995, p. xi).

The fields of education and teacher preparation are at a crossroad. First, it is widely documented that poor and ethnically diverse children achieve at significantly lower levels in our public schools. Second, the composition of today's teaching force is becoming more and more unlike and unfamiliar with the diverse populations in the schools. In spite of the enormous social changes in our society, there has been little change in the teaching that goes on in our schools and in the education of teachers at the university level. In fact, a major shortcoming of teacher education at the university level is that of ill-preparing future teacher candidates in how to successfully meet the needs of diverse children in our schools.

Today, more than ever before, classrooms represent multiracial, multicultural, and multiethnic backgrounds. Many classrooms today have students representing more than a dozen languages as well as many ethnic and racial backgrounds. This situation is only increasing, as two-thirds of the world's immigration now comes to the United States. Teachers in today's classrooms have a responsibility to recognize and appreciate the diversity in children, then capitalize on it by providing excellent, personalized instruction to all children. Only through direct and thoughtfully planned university experiences can future teachers be prepared to be successful in meeting the needs of the diverse populations they will undoubtedly be hired to teach.

The problem of bridging the gap between the school and the world outside is an urgent one. In order to acquire a multicultural perspective, future teachers first need the opportunity to personally examine their own ways of thinking, valuing, believing, and interacting in the world. By careful reflection, guided practice to explore the limitations of individual perspectives, and taking action to restructure personal beliefs, preservice teachers can move toward a multicultural perspective. Finally, to function effectively in multicultural classrooms and schools, educators need to acquire an understanding of the meaning of cultural and ethnic diversity, to examine and clarify their racial and ethnic attitudes, and to develop the pedagogical knowledge and skills needed to work effectively with students from diverse cultural and ethnic groups.

Multicultural education is an education for freedom (Parekh, 1986) within a pluralistic society that should affirm and assist students to understand their home and community cultures. It should also free them from those cultural boundaries in order to be academically successful in schools. Each of us can become culturally encapsulated through socialization while growing up within our communities. During this period, we generally accept the beliefs, assumptions, misconceptions, stereotypes, and values of our own community culture and internalize these. Mainstream students, who comprise the bulk of today's teacher educators, rarely have an opportunity to identify, question, and challenge their cultural perspectives because the school culture usually reinforces those beliefs that they learned at home and in their communities (Banks, 1994). As a result, future teachers from these backgrounds have few opportunities to become free of cultural assumptions and perspectives that are monocultural. Indeed, such viewpoints can devalue, marginalize, or victimize people of color, the poor, or others who are diverse in various ways.

By exploring the relationship between cultural diversity and classroom teaching, student teachers can better bridge the gap for effective schooling of all students. This approach reflects the view expressed by Banks (1991) that teachers must be engaged in a proactive knowledge construction process. Pause and Reflect: Self-Monitoring Activity 1.1 (pp. 7–8) offers an opportunity to illuminate the degree to which cultural beliefs can affect an education that is multicultural.

By now, it is assumed that through the use of the previous activities, preservice teachers have begun an awareness of how prior experiences with family, community, peers, and social groups have developed their beliefs about other cultural groups. In a larger sense, these perspectives are the framework from which they will operate as future teachers unless they restructure their views to include an acceptance/appreciation for diversity with an affirmation of cultural identity through culturally responsive instruction.

The Role of Culturally Responsive Instruction

Culture is learned, shared, adapted, and continually changing. It usually evolves around a system of values, beliefs, and standards which guide people's thoughts, feelings, and behavior (Au, 1993; Hernandez, 1990; Spindler & Spindler, 1990). A culture has physical aspects, such as buildings, clothing, and works of art, and mental or behavioral aspects, such as beliefs about raising children or standards for politeness (Philips, 1983). Culture is learned, because individuals are not born knowing their culture but are socialized into it through the actions of family members and community. Because it is socially constructed, each individual's understanding may be different from another's. Culture is also shared. Members of a cultural group have a common understanding of ways of thinking and ways of behaving. Individuals within a cultural group may adapt to their natural environment or to particular political and economic conditions. Finally, culture is continually changing. Change may be as minor as a new hairstyle or dress code. It can be as dramatic as a long-term trend such as the replacement of industrial workers by robots (Au, 1993).

There are some educators who believe that differences between cultures are trivial and that all people are basically the same. It is for this reason that many reject information about cultural differences because they may equate these generalizations with stereotyping. Yet, knowledge and awareness of cultural differences along with teachers getting to know their individual students' special qualities and backgrounds will alleviate such stereotyping and allow for generalizations that apply in many, but not necessarily all, cases. All students deserve the best educational experiences that schools have to offer, but, in general, students of diverse backgrounds are offered lower-quality educational experiences than students of mainstream backgrounds (Allington, 1991).

The ability to self-reflect and honestly analyze their personal autobiographies allows preservice teachers to understand the importance of instruction that is consistent with the values of their students' own cultures. It is critical that student teachers realize that they do not really see through their eyes or hear through their ears, but through their beliefs. To put beliefs on hold is to cease to exist for a moment—and that is not easy. Such a perspective is called culturally responsive instruction. It means instruction becomes a viable synthesis of perspectives. It is a different orientation and expectation of the whole educational process. A primary goal of this type of instruction is the facilitation of successful learning for all students.

Why have U.S. schools been so much less successful in educating students from diverse backgrounds compared to students from mainstream backgrounds? As Ogbu (1987) and Fordham (1991) point out, students of diverse backgrounds often feel they must choose between being successful in school and being true to their own cultural identities. If teachers use culturally responsive forms of instruction that build upon the students' active knowledge or experience, however, they will assist students to be

Pause and Reflect: Self-Monitoring Activity 1.1

Cultural Autobiography

Think-Pair-Share Portfolio Writing Activity

1. Think about and construct a personal history of your beliefs, assumptions, and values for education and teaching by responding to the following inquiries. Be specific and provide examples for your thinking.

    a. What do you view as the role of schooling?

    - Describe the educational background of parents, grandparents, guardians, or significant other(s).

    - Identify the attitudes and values of parents, grandparents, guardians, or significant other(s) toward education.

    - Describe the support provided by parents, grandparents, guardians, or significant other(s).

    b. What was the relationship between the schools you attended and your experiences with diverse populations?

    - Describe the composition of the elementary and secondary schools you attended, including socioeconomic status, cultural, racial, linguistic, religious, academic, gender, and disability diversity.

Continued

- Identify significant positive and negative experiences of teacher role models in elementary and secondary schools, including ethnicity of the teachers.

- Describe your academic, social, and extracurricular school experiences, including issues of diversity for the groupings, accomplishments, and failures.

c. What do you think about teaching in multicultural classrooms?

- Identify the nature of the community where you lived when you attended elementary and secondary schools.

- Identify the nature of the communities where you have participated in field-based experiences.

- Identify personal experiences you have had with persons from other cultural groups.

2. Pair up with another student and share what has been written. Consider the similarities and differences of your perspective and theirs. Explore and discuss what you see as some implications of these beliefs for instruction in a multicultural classroom.

3. Using this information, develop a personal autobiography to highlight events that may have shaped your professional perspective about teaching in general and about teaching diverse groups of students.

academically successful while still taking pride in their own cultural identity. In addition, by valuing the students' diverse cultures, teachers can capitalize on the strengths and challenges of students.

Another way of thinking about this is to recognize that in going from the community into the school, students of diverse backgrounds must move from one world to another (Phelan, Davidson, & Cao, 1991). If teachers can utilize patterns of instruction that enable students to participate actively and constructively, students are better able to be academically successful. For example, Donna, a Mexican American high school student who maintained a C average, found it difficult to cross the boundaries between the world of school and the world of family and peers. Donna did well in classrooms where teachers communicated a sense of caring about her as an individual and where instruction was built on standards and behaviors valued in her world of family and peer (e.g., putting the group above the self, empathizing with others, being a good mediator). In these classes where teachers used approaches based on discussion, the sharing of ideas, and cooperative learning, the teachers saw Donna as a model student. In contrast, Donna did poorly in classes where instruction was teacher-centered, interaction among students was discouraged, and a passive style of learning was expected. Teachers in those classes hardly knew Donna at all (Au, 1993).

Beyond the mismatches between the culture of the home and the culture of the school are the larger historical, political, economic, and social forces of inequality. Grouping, tracking, and testing are three pervasive examples of this structural inequality. From this point of view, schools may function primarily to maintain the status quo, not to provide all students with a high-quality education. For example, in many elementary school classrooms a disproportionate number of students from diverse backgrounds ends up in the remedial and/or learning disability settings while disproportionate numbers of students from mainstream backgrounds are placed in the gifted education programs. In middle and high schools, students from diverse backgrounds tend to be tracked into vocational programs, while students from mainstream backgrounds tend to enter college preparatory programs.

The use of culturally responsive instruction does not involve a simple matching of instruction to cultural features but is also a matter of adjusting and adapting instruction to meet the needs of all students. It requires a departure from familiar patterns of instruction and a willingness to utilize newer patterns. Special steps are taken to make sure that all students have access to learning and students are never excluded from participation because of their cultural backgrounds. In short, the teacher seeks instructional approaches that work with the majority of students in the class and supports all students in becoming successful within these approaches. Finally, changes in the content of the curriculum, which reinforce students' cultural identities and give them an appreciation for other cultures, appear to be beneficial to all students. Pause and Reflect: Self-Monitoring Activity 1.2 (pp. 11–12) examines your concepts of culture and allows you to reflectively compare these to the thoughts of others.

Thinking Like a Teacher: Recap of Major Ideas

- Critical to the preparation of a perspective of education that is multicultural is an awareness of the enormous demographic changes in the United States.

- The schooling of students of diverse backgrounds can no longer be viewed as an issue to be addressed through special or remedial programs that target at-risk students in each school.

- A major shortcoming of teacher education at the university level is that of ill-preparing our future teacher candidates in how to successfully meet the needs of diverse children in our schools.

- Only through direct and thoughtfully planned university experiences can future teachers be prepared to be successful in meeting the needs of the diverse populations they will undoubtedly be hired to teach.

- To function effectively in multicultural classrooms and schools, educators need to acquire an understanding of the meaning of cultural and ethnic diversity, to examine and clarify their racial and ethnic attitudes, and to develop the pedagogical knowledge and skills needed to work effectively with students from diverse cultural and ethnic groups.

- Multicultural education is an education for freedom within a pluralistic society that should affirm and assist students to understand their home and community cultures as well as free them from those cultural boundaries in order to be academically successful in schools.

- Culture is learned, shared, adapted, and continually changing; it usually evolves around a system of values, beliefs, and standards which guide people's thoughts, feelings, and behaviors.

- Culturally responsive instruction, a viable synthesis of perspectives, is a different orientation and expectation of the whole educational process to facilitate successful learning for all students.

- The use of culturally responsive instruction does not involve a simple matching of instruction to cultural features but is also a matter of adjusting and adapting instruction to meet the needs of all students.

- Changes in the content of the curriculum, which reinforce students' cultural identities and give them an appreciation for other cultures, appear to be beneficial to all students.

Pause and Reflect: Self-Monitoring Activity 1.2

Concepts of Culture

How would you define the culture in which you live? Develop a list of at least five highlights of this culture that characterize it best, in your opinion. Your list items may include values, events, people, places, or things both past and present that you consider culturally significant. Compare your list with those of your classmates. Make a separate list of all the items others selected that are surprising or unknown to you. Why do you think these items were not on your list?

• Definition of culture

• Five highlights of your culture

• Items from your peers not on your list

Continued

• Why were these items not on your list?

Chapter TWO

Components of the Student Teaching Semester

Your student teaching experiences are the culminating activities of your teacher education program. Follow-up studies show that graduating students continue to rate their student teaching experiences as the most beneficial of their entire teacher education program. It is during this time that you are given sample opportunities to integrate knowledge, skills, techniques, attitudes, and methods of behaving in performing as a teacher in a real situation. The purpose of this chapter is to highlight those essential components or characteristics of the student teaching experience that you need to know before you begin in order for the experience to be the success that you expect. To this end, this chapter will cover the areas of student teaching dilemmas, interpersonal relationships, roles of the significant individuals in the experience, the process of gradually learning to teach, and the legal status of student teachers.

Student Teaching Dilemmas

To be successful in your classroom experience, it is helpful to receive some advance knowledge of common pitfalls experienced by student teachers going before you. Three major dilemmas you will face are adjusting to

1. Someone else's classroom
2. A group of diverse students
3. A new time clock in which you must not only "be there" but "be on" at 8:00 A.M. or earlier every morning

Dilemma #1

You have successfully negotiated numerous hurdles in your teacher education program (entrance requirements, GPA minimums, professional course requirements, early field experiences, and personal-family responsibilities) and you have finally made it to your culminating student teaching experiences. Your student teaching coordinator(s) has carefully selected a placement for you to spend the better part of an entire semester learning the teaching role. However, this location is officially the classroom of your supervising teacher and you are a guest in that classroom and school. You must adjust yourself to someone else's classroom, including the physical environment, classroom schedule, style of management and organization, classroom materials, and students. You must (with your supervising teacher's help) adjust and make this classroom yours as quickly as possible. You will be able to accomplish this goal but the reality is that it is your supervising teacher's classroom. Your supervising teacher is the primary authority in the classroom (the students will know this). You will gradually take control of the classroom and then you will experience the comfortable feeling of "ownership." This will take time but you must take the initiative and accomplish this "ownership." It is crucial for your success that you assume the co-teaching role in the classroom, accept the realities of the classroom, and take advantage of your classroom environment in developing your teaching expertise. You must not belabor the reality that the classroom is not officially yours and move forward immediately. Your students will know you are there in a co-teaching role and your supervising teacher will do everything possible to make you feel at home in the classroom. Accepting this reality of adjusting to someone else's classroom and making specific plans should include calling the school and arranging with your cooperating teacher to tour the school and visit her or his classroom. If this can be arranged, be sure to meet with the school principal and secretary and let them know how excited you are to be completing your student teaching in their school. During your classroom visit, try to be helpful in small ways, interact with the students, and note the room arrangement, including doors, windows, bulletin boards, desks, tables, bookcases, cabinets, closets, computers, and special areas. To aid in adjusting to your new environment, complete Pause and Reflect: Self-Monitoring Activity 2.1 (p. 17) by informally interviewing your supervising teacher.

Dilemma #2

The obvious necessary ingredient in your teaching environment (and why you are there in the first place) is students. You have been a student yourself for many years and certainly remember being a member of a group of students during each of your years in school. What could possibly be difficult about getting to know and teach a group of students? First, you have not selected these students to spend your semester with and you must be concerned with all of them, not only the academically motivated students but those who seem unmotivated and undisciplined. Second, you most likely will be in a classroom made up of students from different linguistic, cultural, and economic backgrounds than your own. From the study of teaching, there is evidence that teacher education programs often do not provide enough attention or modeled instruction for working with diverse populations and many times teachers have limited knowledge about cultural, socioeconomic, and linguistic groups different from their own (Avery & Walker, 1993).

It is gratifying to work with students who are eager to learn and who seem to appreciate your efforts in planning meaningful learning opportunities. Yet, due to a variety of factors, there are many students who are not succeeding in school and are not motivated to learn. They may exhibit low self-concepts and may not show appreciation for your efforts. It is frustrating to face this reality each day. You are challenged to embrace these academically diverse students and teach them what they need to know. Also, as discussed in Chapter 1, many students in your classroom will be different from you. You must realize that differences in students may affect your expectations and subsequent teaching actions, but difference does not mean deficit in every case. Again, you are challenged to accept and to embrace students from diverse linguistic, cultural, and economic backgrounds. Your attitudes will greatly affect your students' attitudes and may affect their learning (i.e., the self-fulfilling prophecy). Kuykendall (1992) reports the following student differences are likely to have an impact on teacher attitudes and expectations:

- Prior student achievement
- Prior student behavior
- Prior student placement
- Socioeconomic status
- Language ability
- Physical attraction
- Gender
- Race/ethnicity (p. 3)

You will need to be consciously aware of the necessity of creating a climate of respecting and valuing differences in your classroom. This climate will help you to create a learning environment in which all students are treated equitably. Dealing with differences is part and parcel of teaching, but initially for teachers-in-preparation this realization can be a shock. Yet, student differences are the primary reason teaching is so exciting and fulfilling. If all students were the same in all respects, teaching would be boring.

To help in getting to know the students in your classroom, engage your supervising teacher in a discussion of the students in the class by completing Pause and Reflect: Self-Monitoring Activity 2.2 (pp. 19–20).

Dilemma #3

A third major dilemma confronting you in your school placement may at first sound commonsensical—you must not only be on time each morning but also be ready to perform immediately. There is no time to gradually warm up and teach. Other adults and, most importantly, students will be there demanding your full attention. Unlike your college schedule (Did you have an 8:00 A.M. class each semester?) where you had the luxury of gradually getting up to full speed, you must be ready to go immediately each day of your student teaching.

Becoming a confident student teacher begins with preparation. That means you have all lesson plans with accompanying materials for the day completed in advance, the teaching steps of each lesson have been rehearsed in your mind the night before, and you are ready to greet your students. You cannot be yourself and interact successfully with students if your lessons are not fully completed and you are rushing to be ready. There can be no slow starts and this takes planning and effort on your part. Just as in sports where it is difficult to come back from a poor first quarter or half, it is even more difficult to turn a teaching day around if you start out at anything less than 110 percent prepared. Your students will sense your unpreparedness and management problems will gradually develop. Additionally, the student learning process and your own learning will suffer.

Pause and Reflect: Self-Monitoring Activity 2.1

Informal Interview with Your Supervising Teacher

1. Tell me about your class.

2. What types of diversity are represented by the students in your class? Demographics? Number of males versus females?

3. What is the range of ability in the class? How are the identified special-needs students served? Are they mainstreamed or in pull-out programs?

4. Is there a specific curriculum plan/guide for each subject or content area? Are there guides that I may review?

Continued

5. Do you use any particular grouping plans? How were these developed?

6. Can I receive a copy of our daily schedule?

7. What can I do to prepare myself for teaching with you?

Pause and Reflect: Self-Monitoring Activity 2.2

Informal Interview Regarding the Students in Your Class

1. What cultural groups are represented in this class and school community?

2. How many students speak a primary language other than English?

3. How well do the students who speak a primary language other than English perform in this school?

4. What are the characteristics of the exceptional students in the class?

Continued

5. What are the diverse socioeconomic levels of the students in the class?

6. What are the learning characteristics of students who do not progress satisfactorily in the class?

7. Are there teaching strategies you use that reflect the students' cultural and socioeconomic backgrounds?

8. Are there materials that reflect a multicultural perspective in the classroom and school building?

Time is your most precious commodity and you must do everything you can to utilize classroom time effectively and efficiently. You must master early morning routines to ensure that you are not only there but ready to go when the students arrive. The reality is that student teaching can be a very stressful time—you may get less sleep, change your eating habits, and certainly change your social calendar. Understand that changes are coming and focus on your growth as a teacher. Finally, this may be the last time in your career that so many people are interested in your personal and professional growth. You must take advantage of this opportunity.

Building for Success: Effective Interpersonal Relationships

A large measure of your success as a teacher-in-preparation will be dependent upon your abilities to be an effective communicator and professional colleague. These abilities will directly affect your success in learning to teach and valuing students from different linguistic, cultural, and economic backgrounds. Your field-experience semesters are the culminating experiences of your teacher education program. During these periods, you will be given ample opportunity to integrate knowledge, skills, attitudes, and ways of behaving in performing as a teacher in a real situation. Luckily, you will not be alone in the schools with no one to turn to for help. A team of professionals have been assembled to help you in reaching your goal.

You will be a member of a cooperating team, including your school-based supervising teacher, university supervisor and/or college faculty, other teachers and supervisors at the school, your peers, and the principal. In order for this cooperating team to be effective, all members must be committed to open communication rather than just "getting through the semester without any problems." It is only through true communication and genuine collegiality that you can develop positively in all aspects of the teaching-learning process. However, the primary responsibility for fostering open communication and collegiality rests with you, the student teacher. Although one would expect your university and school-based supervisors to immediately set in motion a true partnership (and this will occur in most instances), you still must take the lead in initiating this teaming process by communicating your willingness to learn as much as possible to your supervisors and your willingness to help your supervising teacher in gradually becoming involved with his or her students as he or she sees fit.

It will only be through numerous open discussions throughout the semester that you will learn and grow as a teacher. Remember, you are there to better learn how to teach and this will automatically necessitate debriefing or sharing sessions with interested parties regarding your strengths, challenges, and growth plans. Unfortunately, many times true communication never occurs and is replaced by just basic civility. To set the stage for open communication and collegiality, the following descriptions of the responsibilities of the cooperating team members are offered as building blocks for a successful semester.

Role of the University Supervisor

Your university supervisor is a special and valuable person in your journey in becoming an educator. He or she is a teacher educator. They have many experiences in teaching at various grade levels, have an intense interest in helping students become teachers, and have been trained to work closely with student teachers in learning the various components of teaching. They will be your sounding board. Listen to them! They will help you grow both professionally and personally throughout your teaching experience. They will be directly involved in your success, giving advice and assistance. They have your best interests at heart at all times, even when they inform you of an error in your ways. It is their job to guide you through this process, helping you integrate university coursework in your teaching, and cooperatively working with your supervising teacher for your success. Specifically, your university supervisor

1. Acts as a liaison person in coordinating the functions of the student teaching experience with the school and the university.
2. Plans and holds seminars for student teachers on timely topics throughout the semester.
3. Assists in the improvement of the student teacher by serving as a coach and counselor.
4. Observes the student teacher as he or she plans and works with students.
5. Provides mentorship opportunities as the student desires.
6. Provides immediate feedback, praise and encouragement, and activities and suggestions which help the student teacher's professional growth.
7. Meets with both the supervisor and the student teacher at different times and in three-way conferences to discuss the needs and development of the student teacher.
8. Completes periodic and final evaluations; writes recommendation letters to school districts or other placement resources.
9. Evaluates the student teacher's portfolios, including lesson and unit plans.
10. Makes recommendations to the university field-experience office concerning initial state certification, withdrawal, reassignment, or extension of the student teaching experience.

Role of the Supervising Teacher

Your supervising teacher is a key person in your successful completion of your student teaching semester. You will spend hundreds of hours with this person learning the teaching role. Your supervising teacher has been carefully selected to work with you by her or his principal and your own student teaching coordinator. Some supervising teachers may receive a small stipend or tuition voucher at your university for working with a student teacher. Yet, the main reason they have agreed to receive you into their classroom and spend hundreds of hours with you for the semester is that they, too, are teacher educators and they derive personal and professional satisfaction in giving back to the profession by sharing their expertise and personally guiding students into the exciting world of teaching. This is not as easy a task as you might expect. They are willing to be a member of the cooperating team (university supervisor, building administrator, and you) and work with new members of the profession. They may spend countless hours with your university supervisor in planning for your success. In addition to consistently demonstrating effective teaching practices at an exemplary level, supervising teachers have been trained as well in how to carefully guide teachers-in-preparation in learning the teaching role. Specifically, the supervising teacher

1. Becomes familiar with the background of the student teacher and introduces the student teacher as a professional coworker to the students and other members of the school staff (e.g., administrators, other teachers, teacher aides, librarians, counselors, support personnel, etc.).

2. Orients the student teacher to the philosophy, curriculum, policies, and special features of the school.

3. Informs the student teacher of the different linguistic, cultural, economic, and achievement backgrounds of the students in the class as well as instructional modifications designed to meet students' needs.

4. Meets during the first week to plan the gradual induction of the student teacher into all facets of the teaching process.

5. Models lessons in each content area, which exposes the student teacher to a variety of teaching materials and techniques.

6. Assists the student teacher in developing effective classroom management techniques.

7. Helps the student teacher plan, teach, and evaluate her or his efforts in each content area.

8. Observes the student teacher frequently, provides immediate feedback on strong areas and areas needing improvement, and cooperatively plans for improvement and growth.

9. Writes midterm and final evaluations of the student teacher's performance and shares these in three-way conferences with the university supervisor and student teacher.

10. Encourages the student teacher to attend parent–teacher conferences, school district staff development programs, and visit other classrooms to observe effective teaching techniques and special programs.

Role of the Building Administrators

As you are well aware, you are a guest in a particular classroom and school in which you are completing the most dynamic phase of your teacher education program. Your school administrators are key individuals and play an important role in possibly gaining a teaching position after completion of your teaching experience. They take a personal and professional interest in you. You are teaching their students. They had input into matching you with your supervising teacher and oversee your experience at the school. Most building administrators will welcome you to their school by giving you a short tour of the school and an explanation of school and district policies, regulations, and rules. They will introduce you to other school personnel, including secretaries, support personnel, and custodial staff. Many principals hold regular meetings with the student teachers in their school around current topics of interest. They will also work cooperatively with your supervisors in resolving any problems that arise in your placement. Depending upon their work load, many principals (if asked by you) will come and observe you teaching various lessons and provide you with valuable written feedback. This will become very important if you desire the building administrator to write a letter of reference and recommend you for a teaching position in the district. Finally, building administrators want you to do well because they know that your success means the students in their school will receive a better education.

Role of the Student Teacher

You are the key person who will decide your success in learning to teach. Learning to teach is a developmentally constructive process based upon your background of experiences, professional background, and your professional attitude. The purpose of this text is to be a part of your becoming an effective teacher for today's diverse classrooms. You will be helped along the way by a team of professionals, but the ultimate person responsible for your success is you. You must take the initiative in meeting your own goals. You have chosen this honorable career path and you should do all that is necessary to be the best teacher you can be for all students. Specifically, the student teacher

1. Attends seminars and staff development meetings throughout the semester given by the school district and university.
2. Conducts oneself in a professional manner.
3. Becomes acquainted with and follows school district policies.
4. Is familiar with the legal responsibilities of student teachers in his or her state (see section on legal responsibilities later in this chapter).
5. Regards information received about students and school personnel as confidential.
6. Becomes aware of, respects, and values students from all cultural, socioeconomic, and language backgrounds.

7. Plans and implements instruction based on students' needs.

8. Adopts a self-improvement learning philosophy, requesting and welcoming constructive suggestions and feedback, and incorporates them into instruction.

9. Attends and participates in parent-teacher conferences, if permitted by the supervising teacher.

10. Seeks out multiple approaches and materials for meeting diverse student needs.

Learning to Teach: The Gradual Increase of Responsibility Model

As a student learning to teach, you should not be given full responsibility of the entire classroom the second or third week of your experience. Do not fear, you will be given ample time to develop your professional teaching skills with lots of support along the way. Each student teaching program and/or classroom supervising teacher has her or his own pacing schedule that takes into account the length of time you will be in your placement and the characteristics of the grade and students, in addition to your own rate of progress. You are there to learn and learning all phases of the teaching role requires observation, small group and individual teaching, and whole class teaching for different subjects or groups in conjunction with your own self-monitoring, reflection, planning, and conferencing with your supervising teacher and university supervisor. In this way, this process of gradually assuming increased responsibility has the underlying theme of "shared thinking about teaching" interwoven throughout the semester. You will gradually assume full responsibility of the entire classroom. The key word here is "gradually." One does not learn how to swim, play golf, use a computer, or pilot a hot-air balloon in a short amount of time. Teaching is far more important and requires a step-by-step thoughtful approach to be successful. You will be carefully guided through this entire process by your supervisors. The increasing responsibility model can be viewed as a pacing schedule that includes your involvement in observing, assisting, small group and team teaching, and whole class teaching (full responsibility) in each subject or area in the curriculum. A description of each aspect of the increasing responsibility model and a visual depiction of this model for an eight-week and sixteen-week experience follows (see Figure 2.1).

Observing—The first activity is that of observing. You will always be required to be a keen observer throughout your career. Early in your student teaching experience you will need to spend more of your time in this important area. These should be focused observations. You not only need to observe your supervising teacher in teaching and managing students in each subject area and in performing noninstructional duties, but also be an observer of the students themselves. Some specific areas to observe during your first weeks in a classroom are student

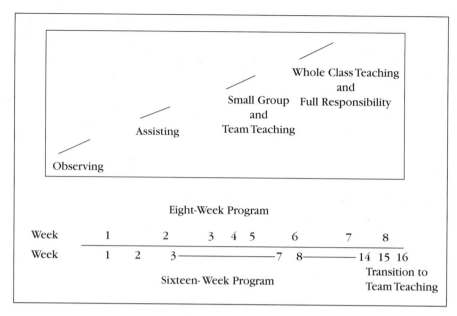

FIGURE 2.1   *Gradual Increase of Responsibility Model*

social interactions, student school behaviors versus social behaviors, transition techniques, pacing of lessons, sequence of events in a lesson, varied teaching techniques, grouping arrangements, and evaluation procedures. After your observations, it is important that you think about what you observed and discuss what you observed with your supervisors as well as your peers.

Assisting—This activity involves helping your supervising teacher in the preparation of lessons and working with individual students. Growth and success in working with small and large groups of students begins with successful one-on-one interactions with students. Assisting your supervising teacher in planning specific lessons will help you down the road when you will be planning and teaching on your own. Other initial activities in which you can assist include keeping attendance, grading papers, passing out materials, aiding students with make-up work, and monitoring student seat work.

Small group and team teaching—Before you assume full responsibility for any group of students, you must have experiences teaching small groups of students on a particular topic and team teaching with your supervising teacher in different subjects. By gradually working with small groups, you will gain the confidence and expertise to be successful with larger groups. Teaming with your supervising teacher can be a most productive and rewarding experience, also. Team teaching involves dividing both the planning and teaching responsibilities in a particular subject. Options for teaming include the student teacher beginning a lesson and the supervising teacher continuing the lesson or vice versa, dividing the class into two groups with each person taking a group for instruction, or one person may present the motivation and readiness for a lesson and the other person direct the guided and independent practice. Rewards can be gleaned from the follow-up discussion of such teamwork. Experiences in both small group and team teaching situations are a wonderful step to being a success in the next area of whole class teaching and full teaching responsibility.

Whole class teaching and full responsibility—At this stage in your teaching experience, you assume full responsibility for all subjects. This is, of course, completed with the support of your supervisors and involves both the planning and teaching of all lessons for all students and fulfillment of all noninstructional duties. Your supervisors are interested in your succeeding in full responsibility and will help you be successful. This will be your time to "fly solo." Your first few weeks in full responsibility will, of course, be stressful and you will have some uncertain times. With your continued efforts and those of your supervisors, however, your remaining weeks of full responsibility will increasingly become more enjoyable, fulfilling, and productive.

Legal Status of Student Teachers

Can you be sued in performing your duties as a student teacher? This is a frequently asked question today pertaining to student teaching. The answer is yes, you can be sued while you student teach. You must always act responsibly and conscientiously in your school placement. Another question is, if legal action is taken against a student teacher, who is responsible for legal costs? The answer in most states (it is recommended that you ask your student teacher director for the specific ruling in your state) is the school district is responsible for providing legal services to student teachers. In most instances, a student who is enrolled in an institution of higher education approved by the state board for teacher training and who is jointly assigned by the institution of higher education and a school board to perform practice teaching under the direction of a regularly employed and certified teacher is accorded the same protection of the laws as that which is accorded the certified teacher while serving as a student teacher. In other words, the student teacher has the same legal responsibility and is accorded the same protection of the laws as the certified teacher. Even in those instances in which the student teacher is alone in the class (the supervising teacher is performing other school-related business) the student teacher is covered under the law. Thus, in most instances, student teachers need not acquire additional liability insurance. If additional liability insurance is required or desired, national teacher associations offer liability insurance as part of student membership to student teachers at a reasonable cost.

It should be noted that in most states, student teachers are not qualified and are not covered under the law to serve as substitute teachers. If the supervising teacher is absent from school, a certified substitute should be appointed as temporary supervising teacher even though the student teacher is directing and teaching the classes at that point in the student teaching experience. Again, this may vary from state to state and you are encouraged to request of your student teaching director the status of substitute teaching in your state.

Thinking Like a Teacher: Recap of Major Ideas

- Student teachers understand and act upon the three major dilemmas of adjusting to 1) someone else's classroom, 2) a group of diverse students, and 3) a new time clock.

- Effective instruction is based upon accepting and valuing students from diverse cultures and linguistic backgrounds.

- A large measure of success in teaching is based upon one's abilities to be an effective communicator and professional colleague.

- It is important to realize the roles and responsibilities of the key individuals in the student teaching experience—university supervisor, classroom supervising teacher, and building administrators.

- The Gradual Increase of Responsibility model includes the process of learning to teach: observing, assisting, small group and team teaching, and whole class teaching and full responsibility.

- It is imperative that you ask your student teaching director what the legal status of student teachers is in your state and ramifications of this finding to your student teaching experience.

- Successful student teachers ultimately take the initiative in meeting their educational goals.

Chapter THREE

Keys to Success
in Student Teaching

The multitude of requirements piled on you as a student teacher is immense. The pressures of the upcoming experience (from yourself, family members, peers, university supervisor, supervising teacher, university director, previous professors, along with a new and demanding time schedule) are enormous. From our many years of working with student teachers, the one question asked most frequently when the topic of student teaching was being addressed was "in what areas do I put my time and energy to ensure I will be successful in my school placement?" In other words, what are the keys to success in student teaching? There is not a more important question at this stage of your development.

It certainly is obvious to anyone connected with student teaching programs that student teachers vary with respect to effort expended in their placement. Unfortunately, some student teachers perform less than the minimum requirements for any number of reasons, probably realizing teaching is not for them at this particular time, and do not finish their placement. A second group of student teachers consists of those who perform the minimum requirements satisfactorily. The third group of student teachers is characterized by the effort of going beyond the minimum requirements in their placement. This group (of which you want to be a member) is identifiable by its members' high degree of commitment to their school placement.

Student teachers in this category plainly work harder before school, during school, and after school. However, not all of these extra efforts are necessarily helpful. Sometimes extra efforts act as "window dressings"— cosmetic but not really very effective. So in what areas should student teachers work hard for success? What specific qualities separate the effective superior student teachers from those who perform only a minimal job? You need to know which efforts are more important than others in student teaching. While acknowledging that no exact formula exists that will ensure success in all instances, we do indeed know many of the characteristics of the effective student teacher. No matter what grade level, method, or class organization, we do know that efforts in the following areas will pay off in student teacher effectiveness (see Figure 3.1):

- Role awareness
- Human relations
- Management and organization
- Gradual induction into full responsibility
- Culturally responsive instruction
- Reflection, evaluation, analysis, and self-monitoring of one's teaching

The key to a successful experience in the schools is the application of a high degree of effort or commitment in these six areas. Student teachers who take the time and effort to grow in each of these areas experience a high degree of satisfaction and success during the course of their time in their school placement. The application of effort in these areas simply makes good sense. The notion of "effort" is optimistic (you can do something about it immediately), unlike the weather, for example, which cannot be manipulated. As you work cooperatively with your supervisors and make

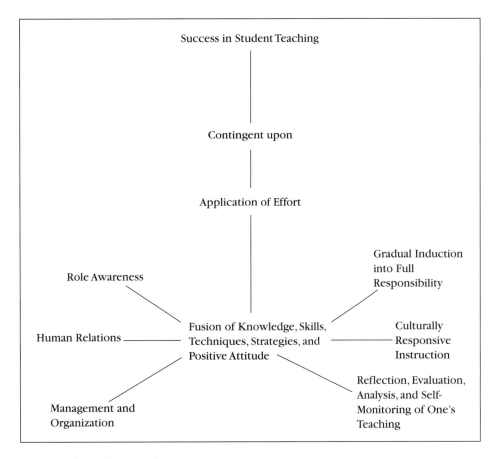

FIGURE 3.1   Keys to Success

use of your good university preparation, it is reasonable to assume your efforts in these specific areas will pay off in success during your placement.

The six knowledge areas along with specific components and possible ways to fulfill each component are presented below. The knowledge areas in and of themselves are not revolutionary nor are the components discoveries. What is distinctive and necessary is the list of possible ways to fulfill each component and *your willingness* to expend effort in each of these areas. It is the actual application of effort in these six areas that is important and you hold the trigger to do this. After reading this section, you are encouraged to reflect on its contents by completing Pause and Reflect: Self-Monitoring Activity 3.1 (pp. 33–34).

Knowledge Area: Role Awareness

Component: Exhibit the ethical responsibilities of the teaching profession.

Possible ways to fulfill this component:

1. Demonstrate a commitment to students by learning about their culture, background, and interests.
2. Maintain the confidentiality of student information.

3. Participate in parent-teacher conferences, after-school workshops, and other professional meetings.

4. Stay abreast of new educational information concerning content areas and teaching trends through discussions with professionals at your school (take written notes and collect information for your professional portfolio).

5. Develop and maintain a positive working relationship with teachers, other school personnel and student teachers, and parents.

6. Develop an appropriate professional relationship with your students.

7. Accept the role of a learner throughout your student teaching experience.

Component: Acknowledge and act upon your influence on individual student development.

Possible ways to fulfill this component:

1. Interact with all students in a fair and honest manner.

2. Accept responsibility to be a professional role model in behavior, personal appearance, and speech.

3. Display a love for learning by sharing personal interests with students.

4. Realize the tremendous impact of negative and positive comments on students.

Component: Recognize and fulfill the noninstructional duties of a teacher.

Possible ways to fulfill this component:

1. Accurately and promptly keep necessary records.

2. Work with students during extracurricular activities.

3. Assume duties of your supervising teacher assigned by the administration (i.e., lunch, hall, bus, etc.).

4. Be available for parent conferences.

5. Develop appropriate communication between home and school.

Knowledge Area: Human Relations

Component: Exhibit positive personal qualities.

Possible ways to fulfill this component:

1. Demonstrate effective character traits such as enthusiasm, consideration, patience, dependability, maturity of judgment, and resourcefulness.

2. Exhibit a sense of humor.

Pause and Reflect: Self-Monitoring Activity 3.1

Logical Analysis of Your Effort

Standing back and looking at your efforts in the student teaching experience is a necessary step after the first few weeks of the experience and should be done periodically throughout the semester. This looking at oneself is essential before looking at other factors at work. The key difference between a student teacher who goes through this process and one who does not is that by looking at your efforts first, you are identifying strengths and challenges to help yourself adjust and grow in your experience.

The Student Teacher Effort Scale, summarizes the six key areas involved in success in student teaching. It is recommended that you rate yourself on each item on the scale by placing a check in the column indicating *how much effort* is expended on each item. This process should be viewed as a nonevaluative way to obtain reasonable information on your progress in student teaching. This information can be shared with your supervisors and/or peers and can be a departure point for reflection and discussion. Rating oneself will encourage one to become more consciously aware of what one is doing or not doing; what areas need to be improved or areas that are satisfactory; and what emphases in your present situation need to be omitted, kept, modified, or expanded. It would be beneficial if you would rate yourself after the first three weeks, seven weeks, twelve weeks, and at the end of your student teaching.

The Student Teacher Effort Scale can be viewed as six action steps needed for success. These steps are optimistic in nature in that they represent something you can do immediately. You have direct control over your attitudes and actions. Each time, after rating yourself, ask yourself the following key question: Are there any discrepancies between where I am and where I would like to be?

Student Teacher Effort Scale

	Strength	Sufficiently Covered	Needs Improvement
1. Role Awareness			
Ethical Responsibilities	_____	_____	_____
Influence on Students	_____	_____	_____
Noninstructional Duties	_____	_____	_____
2. Human Relations			
Personal Qualities	_____	_____	_____
Co-worker and Learner Role	_____	_____	_____
Sharing Relationship with Supervising Teacher	_____	_____	_____
3. Management and Organization			
Functional Physical Environment	_____	_____	_____
Daily Routines	_____	_____	_____
Discipline Techniques	_____	_____	_____

Continued

	Strength	Sufficiently Covered	Needs Improvement
4. Gradual Induction into Full Responsibility			
Transition from Student to Teacher	_____	_____	_____
Assumption of Teaching Responsibilities	_____	_____	_____
5. Culturally Responsive Instruction			
Scope and Sequence	_____	_____	_____
Planning	_____	_____	_____
Assessment	_____	_____	_____
Variety of Teaching Methods	_____	_____	_____
6. Reflection, Evaluation, Analysis, and Self-Monitoring			
Receive Feedback Positively	_____	_____	_____
Monitor Own Progress	_____	_____	_____

3. Demonstrate efficient use of time.
4. Use common sense.
5. Show a willingness and ability to adapt to changes or disruptions in classroom routines.
6. Maintain your good health and vitality.

Component: Accept your role as a co-worker and learner.

Possible ways to fulfill this component:

1. Take the initiative and make decisions.
2. Realize the experience will be a learning situation for you and your supervising teacher.
3. Do not be overly concerned with every detail at the beginning of your experience.
4. Accept the fact that you will make mistakes and have lessons that will be less than perfect.

Component: Develop a sharing relationship with your supervising teacher.

Possible ways to fulfill this component:

1. Share your personal background and educational philosophies.
2. Share teaching materials, ideas, strategies, and techniques.
3. Collect in your portfolio ideas and materials from all levels of content areas of your school.
4. When problems occur, go to your supervising teacher and ask for help.

Knowledge Area: Management and Organization

Component: Develop and maintain a functional physical environment.

Possible ways to fulfill this component:

1. Seek help from your supervising teacher to organize time, space, materials, and equipment for meeting instructional goals.
2. Arrange the classroom to meet the physical and emotional needs of the students.
3. Seek to develop a community of learners in the physical climate.

Component: Implement efficient daily routines and procedures.

Possible ways to fulfill this component:

1. Establish procedures and routines that are easily followed and that minimize disorder and wasted time.

2. Plan ahead as to how you will make transitions from one activity to another.
3. Have all materials ready and available for every activity.
4. Follow school-mandated procedures.
5. Experiment with various ways to get students on-task.

Component: Develop a repertoire of effective discipline techniques.

Possible ways to fulfill this component:

1. Ask your supervising teacher to explain his or her philosophy on classroom discipline and how she or he maintains effective control in the classroom.
2. Learn alternative discipline techniques from other teachers in the school.
3. Maintain reasonable standards of behavior.
4. Demonstrate a variety of positive and negative verbal and nonverbal reinforcers.
5. Work to detect student misbehavior in its early stages and prevent little problems from developing into big ones.

Knowledge Area: Gradual Induction into Full Responsibility

Component: Make the transition from university student to student teacher.

Possible ways to fulfill this component:

1. Call and visit your school before the semester begins.
2. Visit with your supervising teacher before the semester begins.
3. Practice driving to your school in the morning before the semester begins.
4. Acquaint yourself with the building, supervising teacher, principal, support staff, and students at the beginning of student teaching.
5. Ask the principal or supervising teacher for important school policies in school/district manuals.
6. Familiarize yourself with classroom routines, daily schedules, seating arrangements, and student names.
7. Ask if there are students who require special considerations or modifications.
8. Always arrive at your school earlier than the required time.

Component: Gradually assume teaching responsibilities.

Possible ways to fulfill this component:

1. Carefully observe your supervising teacher teaching all subjects, noting teaching strategies and management techniques.
2. As early as possible, assist with routine tasks (i.e. passing out materials, taking roll, collecting materials) and help individual students with their assigned work.
3. Participate in small-group instruction and team teach with your supervising teacher.
4. Assume responsibility for a single subject or period.
5. Work cooperatively with your supervising teacher in gradually teaching additional subjects or periods until full responsibility is assumed.

Knowledge Area: Culturally Responsive Instruction

Component: Familiarize yourself with the scope and sequence of the curriculum.

Possible ways to fulfill this component:

1. Ask to see state and local scope and sequence charts.
2. Examine the curriculum guide(s) and ask how it is used in planning culturally responsive instruction.

Component: Become knowledgeable about your students.

Possible ways to fulfill this component:

1. Review the characteristics and needs of students at a given age or developmental level within various cultural groups.
2. Learn relevant cultural, ethnic, linguistic, personal, and academic background information about individual students.
3. Utilize knowledge about students in motivating and working with them.
4. Check to make sure you are communicating on the students' level of understanding.
5. Promote a positive self-concept in your students.
6. Identify teaching strategies that tend to complement the learning styles of your students.
7. Provide an atmosphere that will encourage students to share home and daily experiences and talk about themselves, their personal interests, and their aspirations.

Component: Understand and participate in the planning process.

Possible ways to fulfill this component:

1. Assist with daily and weekly planning of instructional activities.
2. Begin making your own daily and weekly plans for your teaching.
3. Visualize how your individual lessons are scheduled and how they might fit into the total program.
4. Inquire about beginning and end-of-year planning procedures (make notes and entries in your portfolio).

Component: Develop knowledge and skills in assessing and diagnosing student abilities.

Possible ways to fulfill this component:

1. Investigate the use of formal and informal testing instruments and techniques with students.
2. Ask to analyze available data with your supervising teacher.
3. Investigate how assessment information is used in making instructional decisions.
4. Use information gathered daily to shape tomorrow's lessons.
5. Find out what the referral process is for special programs.

Component: Implement a variety of effective teaching methods to meet the varied needs of students.

Possible ways to fulfill this component:

1. Demonstrate the direct teaching of a particular skill or strategy.
2. Demonstrate the teaching of a problem solving or inquiry objective.
3. Discuss with your supervising teacher the many ways to teach all students in your class.
4. Utilize materials, grouping plans, and teaching strategies that capitalize on the learning styles of diverse learners.
5. Try out different materials and resources to fulfill your teaching objectives.
6. Try out different ways to have productive discussions with your students around a particular theme or topic.

Knowledge Area: Evaluation, Analysis, and Self-Monitoring of One's Teaching

Component: Receive feedback in a constructive manner.

Possible ways to fulfill this component:

1. Ask your supervising teacher for specific feedback on the strengths and challenges of your daily lessons and procedures and interactions with students.

2. Receive all feedback in a positive light.

3. Prepare your individual lessons and unit plans well in advance so your supervising teacher can evaluate them before you teach them.

4. Try to implement each suggestion your supervisors make to you in your teaching and interacting with students.

5. Ask for periodic updates on your progress from your supervising teacher and your university supervisor.

Component: Recognize the importance of self-evaluation and self-monitoring.

Possible ways to fulfill this component:

1. Show a willingness to receive comments and/or suggestions about your performance from your supervisors and building principal.

2. Use and encourage others (supervisors, administrators, fellow student teachers) to use a variety of ways to critique your lessons and performance such as oral and written feedback, audio and video-tapes, and various coding schemes.

3. Keep a teaching diary or log noting improvements in each subject.

4. Continuously ask yourself the questions, "Why am I doing what I am doing?," "What changes can I make to my lesson to make it more motivating and successful?," and "What have I learned today that will help my teaching be more successful tomorrow?"

Thinking Like a Teacher: Recap of Major Ideas

- Successful student teachers realize that where they put their time and effort in teaching relates directly to their effectiveness.
- The application of a high degree of effort is required in the areas of 1) role awareness, 2) human relations, 3) management and organization, 4) gradual induction into full responsibility, 5) culturally responsive instruction, and 6) reflection, evaluation, analysis, and self-monitoring of one's teaching.
- It is important to be aware of and monitor your progress in these six crucial areas throughout your student teaching experience.

Part II

Learning to Teach in Diverse Classrooms

Principles of Effective Instruction

If as future teachers you are to meet the individual needs of students from diverse cultures and linguistic backgrounds, you must have a solid foundation in the knowledge of learning and in the teaching process itself. Each of the remaining chapters deals with one principle of instruction that comes from studying teaching. You as a teacher-in-preparation should realize that your commitment to teaching is crucial; more important, you should be aware of the areas in which your efforts should be spent. The following principles of instruction provide a foundation by specifying seven areas of concern. Thus, the quality of life for all students and academic achievement can be enhanced when teachers do the following:

1. Utilize student feelings and emotions.
2. Provide culturally sensitive classroom management.
3. Provide culturally responsive instruction.
4. Maximize the use of classroom time to teach students what they need to know.
5. Assess student strengths and challenges, provide instruction based on student needs.
6. Use a variety of materials to teach what their students need to know.
7. Believe in their abilities as teachers to make a difference and convince their students that they will learn.

These seven principles of instruction emphasize processes of teaching, processes about which you can gather information while observing and teaching in a classroom. These principles should not be accorded the status of universal truths for all students, all content areas, and all grade levels. Just the opposite is true—you will be able to implement these principles successfully in different amounts depending upon the students in your class, the content you are teaching, the grade level you are teaching, and your style and personality. Each teacher has a particular style; your job is to shape your style to be effective in your own situation. Remember, though effective teachers have different styles, they can produce the same positive results. To become a professional decision-maker you will need to have a healthy attitude toward any teaching strategy and monitor that strategy's effect on students. Because teacher judgment is the key to effective instruction, it is important to give these principles close scrutiny, to experiment with them, and to modify them depending on your situation.

Chapter FOUR

Affective Engagement

> The future of the nation is on the shoulders of teachers and how they teach kids; the future of the world is in the classroom where the teachers are. If we have any chance to guarantee a positive bridge to the twenty-first century, it is how we educate the children in the classrooms today.
>
> —*Richard Green*

The phrase "all children can learn and at high levels" has become something of a cliche among educators in these times of educational reform and school restructuring. The implication here is that if teachers are knowledgeable, skillful, exciting, and caring, then all students will be able to achieve. However, there is a greater need in this culturally pluralistic society for teachers also to view themselves as educators who welcome, adapt, nurture, celebrate, and challenge every student relative to their differences as well as their similarities. An important part of the change process is the ability to acknowledge that no one will know all the answers—something that may be difficult for teachers who are comfortable in the role of content authority and hesitant to relinquish that position. But, as teachers better examine how they can assist students in developing positive self-perceptions as well as curriculum concepts, the affective and cognitive learning experiences for all students can become authentic, long-lasting, and worthwhile.

Since the time of Socrates, educators have argued for a kind of teaching that does more than impart knowledge and teach skills. Life-long learning and real teaching involve helping students understand, appreciate, and grapple with important ideas while developing a depth of understanding in a wide range of issues. Thus, the challenge is for an educational experience that contains breadth as well as depth. Teaching aimed at these important goals is presently most notable for its absence from U.S. classrooms. As important as skills and knowledge undoubtedly are, no less important are more effectively demanding learning opportunities that promote "enlarged understanding of ideas and values" (Adler, 1982).

Goodlad (1984) reports that:

> A great deal of what goes on in the classroom is like painting-by-numbers . . . (teachers) ask for specific questions calling essentially for students to fill in the blanks: "What is the capital city of Canada?" . . . Students rarely turn around by asking questions. Nor do teachers often give students a chance to romp with an open-ended question such as "What are your views on the quality of television?" (p. 108).

For the culturally diverse learners, this means that "they" (diverse learners) must become "we" (a community of learners). Many students have given up hope in themselves due to an inability to see themselves as part of that community of learners. As educators, however, we must not give up hope in them and their potential. Critical to this perception is the belief that the teacher is the single most significant factor in determining whether students will be successful in learning. In fact, the most important learning for culturally and linguistically diverse students is that mediated by people—their teachers and their peers.

Student Self-Perceptions

Since feelings are clearly linked to student learning, the first step in looking at the teaching process is a review of the importance of self-perception in learning. According to Beane and Lipka (1986), self-perceptions have two dimensions: 1) *self-concept*, which is "the description an individual attaches to himself or herself" (p. 5), and 2) *self-esteem,* which refers to "the evaluation one makes of the self-concept description and, more specifically, the degree to which one is satisfied or dissatisfied with it, in whole or in part" (p. 6). The authors further describe the two broad influences in forming self-perceptions, which are the individual self and one's environment. Factors influencing the individual self include one's values and beliefs, assumptions about one's self and other people, attitudes, and needs. Environmental factors that have a major influence on one's self-perceptions include the home, the classroom itself, the curriculum, other people (both in and out of school), and, most important, the teacher. Of course, these factors have been at play since birth and are constantly interacting.

The implications for teaching include the belief that students who feel good about themselves are not afraid to learn something new and are interested in new experiences, whereas students who have developed negative self-perceptions are less confident and do not feel worthy. Thus, these students are often not open to new experiences in school because they perceive of these experiences as another opportunity to fail. An individual's approach to any activity is influenced by prior experiences and his or her accumulated perceptions of such activity. Even though changing a student's negative self-perception is not easy, it can be accomplished over time by a caring, enthusiastic teacher who utilizes culturally responsive instruction.

Since learning is not just a matter of skill or cognitive strategies but a matter of will or feelings and emotions (Winograd & Paris, 1988), much depends on the teacher's ability to provide opportunities for learning that students find meaningful and interesting. The idea of affective engagement is especially important when it comes to the instruction of students of diverse backgrounds. The social contexts of the environment (e.g., home and community) often prepare students of diverse backgrounds to learn in ways quite different from those expected by the school. Admittedly, there is not just one way to read or just one way to write and understand the world; the literate person is one who can read, write, and understand in ways that meet the requirements of the various social contexts in his or her worlds. For example, in a study of an elementary school in a diverse neighborhood of Philadelphia, Gilmore (1983) discovered that students used literacy in particular ways that teachers did not acknowledge or value as authentic. One instance of this existed when students wrote notes to one another, but teachers did not see the composing of these notes as writing. Similarly, teachers did not recognize the spelling and decoding skills girls showed when they participated in "doin' steps," a distinctive type of street rhyme among African American females. Gilmore concludes that, because only officially sanctioned activities count as literacy in school, teachers are often unaware of the full range of literacy learning skills that culturally and linguistically diverse students may possess. Gilmore's research indicates the powerful relationship between teachers and students for the endorsement of some forms of learning and the dismissal of others. The implications are clear—for culturally responsive instruction, teachers need to be aware that learning may take many forms. While teachers will want to acquaint all students with mainstream forms of cognitive skills, they will also want to be aware that various other forms of literacy may be significant in the lives of students of diverse backgrounds. This type of affective engagement helps to shape the students' self-perceptions and self-esteem, which influences the quality of learning that may or may not take place for the student. Pause and Reflect: Self-Monitoring Activity 4.1 (p. 47) is designed to help you focus on some of the unique but diverse ways that you use literacy daily.

Student Needs and Affective Teaching

What makes some students more successful in learning than others? This seems to be an age-old question for schooling as it is presented in this country. Certainly self-perception and self-esteem play key roles. Another powerful factor is the fulfillment of personal needs. According to this concept, a person performs according to his or her perceived needs in the classroom. Students and adults generally act in ways that make sense to themselves. The best learning occurs when a student both feels a need to know something and believes he or she has a reasonable chance at success. Within a society that values education that is multicultural so that students from all social, racial, cultural, and gender groups will have an equitable opportunity to learn, school reform is now targeted on multiple perceptions of school success. These should include attitudes, values, beliefs, and actions of the school staff; formalized curriculum and course of study; learning, teaching, and cultural styles favored by the school; languages and dialects of the school; instructional materials; assessment and testing procedures; the school culture; the "hidden curriculum;" and the counseling program (Banks, 1994). Since students have different needs, teachers must learn to recognize these needs and try numerous options when interacting with students.

Abraham Maslow (1943), the distinguished psychologist, proposed a theory of motivation based on fundamental human needs. Maslow viewed human needs in relationship to others and in a bottom-to-top hierachy. He theorized that one's need seems to monopolize a person's attention until that need is satisfied. His hierarchy of needs had five levels: physiological, safety, love and belonging, self-esteem, and self-actualization. Maslow's levels and descriptors for each are presented in Figure 4.1. The increase of cognitive abilities occurs in the self-actualization stage. However, if needs are largely not met in other stages, it is unlikely that much success in the cognitive area can be achieved, since all needs are both interrelated and interdependent.

Pause and Reflect: Self-Monitoring Activity 4.1

Portfolio Entry

What are some of the major ways you, your family, and friends use literacy in everyday life? To answer this question, keep notes for a week on your own literacy activities, as well as the literacy activities of your family and friends. Share your findings with another student who has participated in this same activity and is culturally or linguistically diverse from you. Develop a Venn diagram to illustrate the similarities and differences that you can discern from your lists of activities.

<u>Venn Diagram</u>

What implications can you make from the findings?

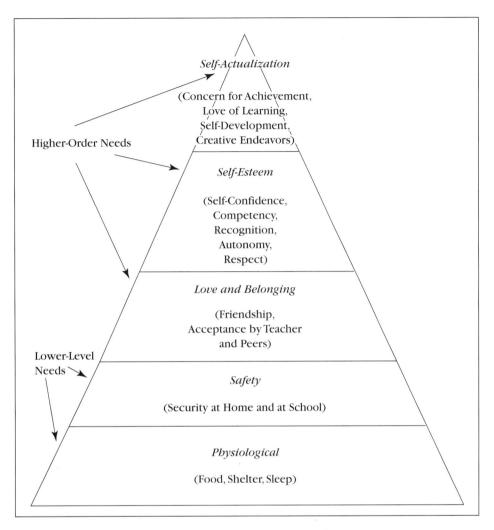

Higher-Order Needs

Lower-Level Needs

Self-Actualization

(Concern for Achievement,
Love of Learning,
Self-Development,
Creative Endeavors)

Self-Esteem

(Self-Confidence,
Competency,
Recognition,
Autonomy,
Respect)

Love and Belonging

(Friendship,
Acceptance by Teacher
and Peers)

Safety

(Security at Home and at School)

Physiological

(Food, Shelter, Sleep)

FIGURE 4.1   Maslow's Hierarchy of Human Needs

Instructional goals will not be fully realized without proper attention to student needs. Furthermore, the fundamental, lower-order needs (i.e., physiological, safety) must be met before teachers can be successful. For example, before a teacher can focus on a student's self-esteem, the student's physiological and safety needs must first be met. Yet, if a student's self-esteem is low, it is unlikely he or she will be motivated to try new things in the classroom. Likewise, if a student is hungry or tired, it is unlikely the student will want to learn or perhaps be able to learn, even if it will help him or her in next year's math class. The key at the self-esteem level, however, is to emphasize competency; that is, that your students are doing the right things and can be successful in your classroom. To allow affective engagement, however, the teacher must be aware that being successful in reading a social studies text is dependent not just on a student's general reading ability. It is also dependent on many instructional factors, including the readability level of the text, the context of instruction or task requirements, and the application of specific skills such as ability to locate the main idea, significant details, sequence of events, and cause/effect relationships. The teacher's ability to enlist student interest and motivation in reading a particular chapter will also affect the student's level of success. This exemplifies the importance of the teacher and the teacher's influence in meeting or not meeting a student's needs. By ascertaining that students have the prerequisite abilities to read a particular social studies chapter, the teacher can fulfill their instructional needs and assist students in succeeding at the next learning task. In this view, one of the best ways to meet students' needs is to offer a sound instructional program that is culturally responsive. There is no substitute or commercial material to replace good teaching, which provides the bridge between basic student needs and instructional needs. Pause and Reflect: Self-Monitoring Activity 4.2 (p. 51) is designed to help you examine your own thinking about the inequities of instruction for culturally and linguistically diverse students.

Emotional Maturity and Affect

Everyone has emotional needs, and they play an important role in the learning process. Raths (1972) hypothesized that students have eight emotional needs: belonging, achievement, economic security, love and affection, sharing and respect, to be free from fear, to be free from intense feelings of guilt, and the need for self-concept and understanding. Students grow in a number of ways, including emotional stability. If our needs are met, we feel good about ourselves and approach new events with confidence; conversely, if emotional needs are not met, Raths hypothesized, this will lead to negative self-esteem and reluctance about and apathy toward undertaking new situations. Thus, our emotions can be manifested in positive and negative ways.

The daily interactions of teachers and students within the classroom environment can promote emotional maturity for the community of learners. Heightened sensitivity and awareness toward all students will directly affect emotional growth as well as cognitive growth. Being able to respond appropriately to students depends on how well you know them, how sensitive you are to their needs, and how able you are to "read" students. The opportunity to grow and learn in a sensitive, nurturing, and supportive environment is all the learner needs for emotional maturity and is exactly what will benefit each and every one. Therefore, your ability to understand students is dependent upon knowing them—not just academically but being acquainted with their interests, needs, likes, dislikes, health, fears, hobbies, and friends. Knowing the students will enable you to respond appropriately in various classroom situations.

Interactional Discourse Styles and Affect

In classrooms throughout the world, but particularly in the United States, teaching events are structured daily around teacher-student dialogues (Garcia, 1992). Typically, the teacher asks a question or requests a student

Pause and Reflect: Self-Monitoring Activity 4.2

Portfolio Entry

Why do you think schools are generally successful with students of mainstream backgrounds, but generally unsuccessful with students of diverse cultural backgrounds? As you reflect on formulating your thinking, try to put ideas from this chapter together with your own ideas and personal experiences.

response. The student then replies. The teacher then evaluates the student's response and may request further elaboration. Such conversations are an instructional strategy in that they are designed to promote learning. Yet, they are structured to take advantage of natural and spontaneous interactions with an affective focus on cognitive concepts. They also allow a high level of participation without undue domination by any one individual, particularly the teacher.

Because many teachers are from mainstream backgrounds, they are less likely to be familiar with the diverse interactional discourse styles of culturally and linguistically diverse learners. In fact, many teachers are unaware that the difficulties they experience when conducting these conversational lessons may be the result of mix-ups in communication that result from differences in style. Instead, teachers may tend to attribute the problems that students experience during lessons to flaws in the students' intellect or character.

For example, a teacher may decide a student is just naturally slow to learn, unmotivated, lazy, or inattentive based on an incongruent interactional discourse style. Clearly, such circumstances fall into the familiar old pattern of "blaming the victim" or assuming that the problem lies within the student rather than in the situation. Differences in interactional discourse styles often need to be bridged in order to bring about culturally responsive instruction. Bridging these differences is one of the affective differences that may allow teachers to work more effectively with students of diverse backgrounds. However, a failure to recognize or acknowledge the existence of differences in interactional styles (e.g., failure to adjust instructional situations) is one of the traditional patterns that appears to prevent students of diverse backgrounds from achieving at high levels in school.

In research conducted by Sarah Michaels (1981; 1986) from the first grade classroom of a teacher called Mrs. Jones, Michaels focuses on "sharing time." Universally, sharing time is part of the school culture for primary grades and generally reflects mainstream expectations and norms for interaction. The teachers use questions and comments to assist children in learning to use discourse much like what they would encounter in books or use when they write. Even though the discourse used by some children may be quite different from the oral language many children bring to school, Cazden (1988) points out that sharing time is one of the few occasions in the school day when children have the chance to talk about their personal experiences and to bring their lives at home into the classroom.

In this particular classroom, half of the students were African American and half were European American. Every day, the teacher (Mrs. Jones) called upon volunteers to give a narrative account about an important event (e.g., a birthday party) or a formal description of some object (e.g., a new coat). Mrs. Jones expected the children to name and describe objects, even those in plain sight, and to assume the audience had little or no background knowledge about the event and its context. One of Mrs. Jones' main requirements was that the children should stick to a single topic (e.g., *topic-centered* style of interaction). Michaels' study demonstrates that the European American children in the class had little difficulty meeting these requirements. Their accounts were focused on a single topic or closely related topics and led to a resolution. The following transcript of one European American female student supports this assumption (pp. 431–432):

Mindy: When I was in day camp we made these um candles.

Teacher: You made them?

Mindy: And uh I—I tried it with different colors with both of them but one just came out, this one just came out blue and I don't know what this color is.

Teacher: That's neat-o. Tell the kids how you do it from the very start. Pretend we don't know a thing about candles. OK. What did you do first? What did you use? Flour?

Mindy: Um . . . there's some hot wax, some real hot wax that you just take a string and tie a knot in it. And dip the string in the um wax.

Teacher: What makes it uh have a shape?

Mindy: Um you shape it.

Teacher: Oh you shaped it with your hand. Mm.

Mindy: But you have, first you have to stick it into the wax and then water and then keep doing that until it gets to the size you want it.

Teacher: Okay, who knows what the string is for?

Michaels concludes that Mrs. Jones was able to collaborate with Mindy by timing her questions so that they occurred just as Mindy had completed a thought. The questions were not perceived by Mindy as an interruption. The level of questions were moved from general to specific with cueing to start the description of making the candles by telling about the materials used. Finally, Mrs. Jones' comments and clarifications built on what Mindy had started to say. With this strategy, Mrs. Jones was able to assist Mindy in following the rules for sharing time and Mindy learned something about how to present an account using literate discourse.

The next account of an African American child in the class indicates a different interactional discourse style where the child attempts to present a series of episodes linked to some person or theme. Mrs. Jones had asked the student to share ". . . one thing that's very important" (pp. 435–436):

Deena: Um. In the summer, I mean, w-when um I go back to school, I come back to school in September, I'ma have a new coat, and I already got it. And it's um got a lot of brown in it. And when um, and when I got it yesterday, and when I saw it my mother was, was goin somewhere, when I saw it on the couch and I showed my sister, and I was readin' something out on, on the bag and my sister said, Deena you have to keep that away from Keisha, 'cause that's my baby sister, and I said no. And I said the plastic bag because um when um sh-when the um she was um (with me), wait a minute, my cousin and her . . .

Teacher:	Wait a minute. You stick with your coat now. I said you could tell one thing. That's fair.
Deena:	This was about my c—
Teacher:	Ok, alright, go on.
Deena:	This was—and today, and yesterday when I got my coat, my cousin ran ouside and he ran to, tried to get him, and he, he, he start—an' when he get in, when he got in my house, he layed on the floor and I told him to get up because he was cryin'.
Teacher:	Mm—what's that have to do with your coat?
Deena:	H-he, because—he wanted to go outside, but we couldn't (exasperated)
Teacher:	Why?
Deena:	Cause my mother wanted us to stay in the house.
Teacher:	What does that have to do with your coat?
Deena:	Bec—um uh.
Child:	(whispers)
Deena:	Because, I don't know.
Teacher:	Ok. Thank you very much, Deena.
Children:	(talking)
Teacher:	Ok, do you understand what I was trying to do with Deena? I was trying to get her to stick with one thing. And she was talking about her . . .
Children:	Coat.
Teacher:	New . . .
Children:	Coat.
Teacher:	. . . coat. It sounds nice, Deena.

Michaels concludes from this discussion that Mrs. Jones provides indications that she did not have the cultural knowledge to understand the *topic-associated* style of this child. She could not discern the topic of the discourse or predict where the child's narrative was headed. As a result, she often mistimed her questions and ended up cutting the child off. The connections in Deena's account (among her cousin, her baby sister, and the coat) are not readily apparent. If Mrs. Jones had been able to collaborate with Deena as she did with Mindy, perhaps Deena would have been able to verbalize the connections. But Mrs. Jones was unable to time her comments appropriately, twice interrupted Deena in the middle of a clause, and she asked Deena questions three times. Deena's train of thought may well have been disrupted by Mrs. Jones' attempts to help her move toward a different style (topic-centered) of sharing. Unfortunately, Deena did not have the opportunity to learn to present her account using literate discourse because Mrs. Jones was unable to build on what Deena was saying.

Later interactions with Deena by Michaels clarified many of the previously unstated connections in her account. According to Deena, her cousin was "a bad little boy" who came into the house with dirty hands, which he started to put on her coat. Her baby sister entered the picture because the plastic bag over the coat might be dangerous; Deena had to keep it away from her. Her coat had caused Deena to be concerned about both her cousin and baby sister, although for different reasons. During interactional discourse, the area of self-esteem could have been hindered if Deena's perception included thoughts that the teacher was not interested in what she had to say. Although far from their intent, teachers may unknowingly send children of diverse backgrounds the message that their experiences are less important than the experiences of other children, or that in some way they are not able to articulate their thoughts in an appropriate manner.

In a discussion with Michaels, another teacher who understood the *topic-associated* style described in the previous situation shared this time of interactional discourse with her student (pp. 114–115):

> Antonia, an African American student in the combination first/second grade class, had composed the following draft:
>
>> "I have a cat and my cat never go to the bathroom when my cousin eating over my house and we went to the circus my cousins names are LaShaun Trinity Sherry Cynthia Dorel." (p. 114).
>
> As Michaels watched, the teacher asked Antonia to read her draft aloud. When the child had finished reading, the teacher responded, "Boy, you've got a lot of cousins!" For the next few minutes she chatted with Antonia about her family. Then the teacher paused and asked in a thoughtful tone, "Just one more thing . . . what do your cousins . . . have to do with the circus . . . and your cat?" Antonia replied confidently, "Oh, my cousins always eat over my house, and they sleep over my house, too. And one day last week, we all went to the circus." "Oooh, I see," said the teacher, nodding her head and smiling. . . . Later the teacher commented to Michaels, "You know, it's a whole lot easier to get *them* to make the connections clear, if you assume that the connections are there in the first place."

Some of the findings in Michaels' research suggests that being aware that cultural differences may exist in interactional discourse (e.g., *topic-associated versus topic-centered* style) is an important step for affective engagement. It is important also for teachers to begin with the assumption that students' actions are inherently logical even though the logic they are following may be quite different from that of the teachers' experiences or teacher preparation.

Affective Engagement with Cultural Differences

Relative to diverse interactional discourse and other differences that may exist, there is a full range of strategies available to teachers and students who must deal with the stress caused by cultural differences or cultural incongruences. Jacob and Sanday (1976) suggest that educators may pursue one of five strategies:

1. Contact with individuals of other cultures is avoided.

2. Contact is kept to a minimum or regulated to areas where differences are minimal.

3. Contact occurs regularly, but misunderstanding and misinterpretation lead to open conflict and hostility.

4. Contact occurs regularly, but the individual changes his or her operating culture to incorporate the standards of the culture of the individuals who hold the balance of power in the contact situation.

5. Contact occurs regularly, and all involved in the interaction work toward the development of a community of learners (p. 98).

The first four strategies place a heavily affective burden on the student. Strategies 1 and 2 make learning new ideas or concepts virtually impossible, because students do not have the opportunity to participate in lessons and to interact sufficiently with teachers. Strategy 3 may lead students to feel threatened and to resist the effects of schooling. Strategy 4 denies the values of diversity and implies that it is only students of culturally and linguistically diverse backgrounds, not teachers and schools, who need to do the learning. An underlying assumption is the acceptance of the dominant culture and a rejection of all others.

Strategy 5 allows teachers and students to work together to create a community of learners by affirming the students' cultural identities, thus permitting them to strive for high levels of literacy and academic achievement. It further allows teachers and students to affirm the value of diversity. This strategy appears to be the only strategy that puts both teachers and students in a win-win situation toward collaboration that ultimately can lead to the development of mutual adaptation for improved opportunities to learn and at high levels. Pause and Reflect: Self-Monitoring Activity 4.3 (p. 59) provides you a chance to explore your teachers' affective engagement with students while challenging you to examine your own perceptions of similar engagements.

Self-Monitoring FYI: "Reading" Students

Definition: The ability to infer students' motivations, interests, and needs through the accumulation of information observed.

Indicators:

- Listen and assess your students' verbal responses for signs of hesitation, confusion, acceptance, self-confidence, motivation, interest, antagonism, and boredom.
- Be sensitive to and aware of nonverbal cues (e.g., facial expressions, physical movements, reactions to peers, and reactions to failure).
- Know students' present level of achievement and specific instructional challenges.
- Know students' interests and develop awareness of their values, backgrounds, and cultures.

- Look for patterns of student responses—always missing the main idea, for instance.
- Notice the students' preferences in learning activities or organizational patterns.
- Translate informed hunches into classroom action; that is, by making changes in instructional programs.

Thinking Like a Teacher: Recap of Major Ideas

- There is a need in this culturally pluralistic society for teachers to view themselves as educators who welcome, adapt, nurture, celebrate, and challenge every student relative to their differences as well as their similarities.
- As teachers better examine how they can assist students in developing positive self-perceptions, the affective and cognitive learning experiences for all students can become authentic, long-lasting, and worthwhile.
- As important as skills and knowledge undoubtedly are, no less important are more affectively demanding learning opportunities to promote the concept of enlarged understanding of ideas and values.
- The social contexts of the environment often prepare students of diverse backgrounds to learn in ways quite different from those expected by the school.
- The best learning occurs when a student both feels a need to know something and believes he or she has a reasonable chance to succeed.
- The daily interactions of teachers and students within the classroom environment can promote emotional maturity for the community of learners.
- The teacher's ability to understand students is dependent on knowing them—not just academically but by being acquainted with their interests, needs, likes, dislikes, health, fears, hobbies, and friends.
- Failure to recognize or acknowledge the existence of differences in interactional styles is one of the traditional patterns that appears to prevent students of diverse backgrounds from achieving at high levels in school.
- Teachers need to be careful that they do not send children of diverse backgrounds the message that their experiences are less important than the experiences of other children, or that in some way they are not able to articulate their thoughts in an appropriate manner.
- It is important for teachers to begin with the assumption that students' actions are inherently logical even though the logic they are following may be quite different from that of the teachers' experiences.
- Teachers must strive to work together with students to create a community of learners by affirming the students' cultural identities.

Pause and Reflect: Self-Monitoring Activity 4.3

Portfolio Entry

To gain insights into the feelings/emotions of students, use the following questions to interview two or three teachers in your school:

1. What are the dominant attitudes and feelings students have in your grade level? Include information that indicates the students' needs, emotions, fears, likes, dislikes, and values.

2. What are some strategies that you use to enhance students' self-esteem?

3. What strategies do you use to motivate students to learn?

4. Do you believe that a teacher can overemphasize a concern for student affect? If so, what examples can you provide?

After evaluating and reflecting on the teachers' responses, decide if this information conflicts with your own experiences and perceptions? If so, to what do you attribute the differences?

Chapter FIVE

Classroom Management

The Importance of Managing the Classroom

Research on teaching has clearly pointed to the teacher's role in improving education. As we shall see in later chapters, your thoughts, judgments, and actions related to teaching methods have a direct bearing on whether or not students are provided an appropriate education. However, you must design and employ effective teaching techniques not for one student exclusively, but for an entire class simultaneously. Thus, in addition to purely "instructional" concerns, you need to be able to create, manage, and maintain an environment conducive to learning. Studies of the concerns of experienced, first-year, and student teachers singled out classroom management as one of the most difficult and stressful elements in teaching (Evertson, Emmer, Clements, & Worsham, 1997). Teachers-in-training and first-year teachers, especially, equated success with the ability to manage the classroom effectively.

Studies have shown that effective instructors are proficient in classroom organization and management (Slavin, 1997). Although they are interrelated and interdependent, managerial abilities need to be differentiated from the instructional abilities of teachers.

A teacher may have highly developed instructional skills in the areas of planning, teaching, and evaluating, but may fail miserably in the classroom because of a lack of managerial skills. Of course the opposite can also be true: A teacher may be highly skilled in classroom management and organization but fail because of poorly developed instructional abilities. Expertise in both areas is required for successful teaching.

Managerial concerns address the need for teachers to provide and maintain classroom conditions conducive to student learning. One only has to observe for a short time in a classroom to have a healthy regard for effective classroom management. Some teachers run such smooth classrooms that you may think management is an innate trait. Clearly it is not, and dealing appropriately with the wide range of student abilities and needs in a classroom is a challenge. As part of your teacher training program, you may have already completed a course on classroom management and studied approaches to classroom discipline. While it is not our intent to focus on a particular discipline method or philosophy, some of the major approaches are listed below. You are encouraged to become familiar with various approaches to help clarify your own philosophy concerning discipline.

Jones, V. F., & Jones, L. S. (1994). *Comprehensive classroom management: Creating positive learning environments for all students.* (4th ed.). Boston: Allyn & Bacon.

Levin, J. & Nolan, J. F. (1996). *Principles of classroom management: A professional decision-making model.* (3rd ed.). Boston: Allyn & Bacon.

Curwin, R. L., & Mendler, A. N. (1988). *Discipline with Dignity.* Alexandria, VA: Association for Supervision and Curriculum Development (ASCD).

Glasser, W. (1969). *Schools without failure*. New York: Harper & Row. Glasser, W. (1986). *Control theory in the classroom*. New York: Harper & Row. Glasser, W. (1990). *The quality school*. New York: Harper & Row.

Wolfgang, C.H. (1995). *Solving discipline problems: Methods and models for today's teachers*. (3rd ed.). Boston: Allyn & Bacon.

Nelsen, J., Lott, L., & Glenn, H.S. (1993). *Positive discipline in the classroom*: Rocklin, CA: Prima Publishing.

Gordon, T. (1974). *Teacher effectiveness training*. New York: David McKay.

Canter, L., & Canter, M. (1976). *Assertive discipline: A take charge approach for today's educator*. Seal Beach, CA: Canter & Associates.

Carkhuff, R. (1983). *A design for discipline: The least approach*. Washington, D.C.: National Education Association.

The recommendations that follow reflect an eclectic view, representing philosophies that range from an affective or personal-growth perspective to an ecological, environmental view to a behavioristic approach. Effective managers generally use a combination of approaches because they have adopted a positive problem-solving attitude toward management. The nature of individual differences precludes the pronouncement of "the one correct way" of managing the classroom. The goal is to set optimal conditions for learning, and there are a multitude of ways to achieve this end. The method you use will depend on the grade level taught, the students, the subject, and the type of learning you are addressing.

Cultural Sensitivity

As you are well aware, students in classrooms today represent a variety of multiracial, multicultural, and multiethnic backgrounds. With respect to classroom management, classroom teachers need to recognize and appreciate the cultural diversity within their classrooms and capitalize on it by providing excellent instruction to all students. This means that one's classroom management is affected by multicultural concerns. Central to achieving a successful management program is knowing your students as individuals and becoming culturally acquainted with their family and community. Fuller (1996) speaks to this very point by stating, "Successful classroom management requires more than a model; it requires cultural sensitivity, because it is impossible for teachers to address the needs of children whose backgrounds they do not understand and appreciate" (p. 141). All teachers need to gather information on students whose backgrounds are different than their own. This gathering of information on your students will lead to specific instructional and management guidelines. Fuller recommends teachers collect information about new cultural backgrounds by researching the answers to the following questions:

1. What is the group's history?
2. What are the important cultural values of the group?
3. Who are the outstanding individuals who claim membership in this group?
4. What are the group's major religions and beliefs?
5. What are the current political concerns?
6. What are the group's political, religious, and social celebration days?
7. What are the educational implications of the answers to the preceding questions? (pp. 153–154).

Every classroom management model should be based on the diversity of students in that classroom. This necessitates teachers learning everything they can about their students. Knowing and valuing differences and building a flexible management style that is culturally sensitive are hallmarks of a true professional.

Elements of Successful Management

As you might suspect, successful classroom managers have relatively few discipline problems because they put their efforts into preventing or reducing the likelihood of trouble occurring in their classrooms. Studies on teaching have identified the teacher's ability to find ways to keep students actively engaged in instructional activities as the key to successful classroom management (Evertson, Emmer, Clements, & Worsham, 1997). Overwhelming evidence points to three clusters of attributes as key elements in achieving the goal of effective classroom management (Heilman, Blair, & Rupley, 1998):

1. Planning of activities
2. Managing of group instruction
3. Monitoring of student progress

There is a positive side to each of these elements: You, the teacher, have direct control over each of them. Through practice and self-monitoring of your growth in this area, you can continue to improve, lesson after lesson.

Planning of Activities

Effective teachers remember the adage that "an ounce of prevention is worth a pound of cure," and systematically prepare for the upcoming school year, planning in advance for individual lessons (Emmer, Evertson, Clements, & Worsham, 1997). Good managers spend time before the school year begins collecting and organizing materials and planning activities to be used with their students. The better the preparation of materials and activities prior to actual teaching, the more confidence you will have in daily interactions with students and the more you can concentrate on actual teaching. Gathering materials at the last minute will eventually wear both you and your students down. Also, prior to the beginning of school and certainly in the first month of school, you will need to collect assessment information on your students to aid in highlighting strengths and areas needing attention. This information will help you in planning effective instruction throughout the year. Both the collection of diagnostic data on students and the collection of materials and activities prior to the beginning of school are considered "preventive" management measures, because spending time on these areas will ensure more meaningful instruction tailored to students' needs and free you of the burden of deciding these matters the day before or "on the spot." Above all, the key to effective classroom management is prevention (Good & Brophy, 1984). Good and Brophy succinctly state, "The key to success lies in the things the teacher does ahead of time to create a good learning environment and a low potential for trouble" (p. 177).

Furthermore, good classroom managers spend time at the start of each school year discussing classroom rules and procedures with their students. Depending on their age and grade level, the rules and procedures can range from rules for lining up for lunch and movement within the room to discussion procedures to rules for the use of hall passes. At each grade level students should have input in determining class rules. Your expectations should be made clear to students, and it is best to model these behaviors with younger children. These rules and procedures need to be reviewed with all students until they know them. By ensuring that these procedures are clear to the students, you will be preventing possible management problems. The following are management suggestions to consider in your preparation before the school year begins:

- Collect as much diagnostic data (i.e., formal and informal) on students as possible.

- Decide on "must" classroom behavior rules and procedures (i.e., those not negotiable with students) regarding tardiness, dismissal, hall passes, makeup work, homework, etc.

- Decide ahead of time how you intend to explain classroom behavior standards and your expectations concerning assignments and classroom procedures.

- Organize and arrange instructional materials for easy access and distribution.

- Plan the seating arrangement to ensure a smooth transition of movement from one activity to another. You should be able to see the whole class from wherever you are stationed when teaching and you will need to monitor students during supervised and independent assignments.

- Check the class roster to determine if any special education students will be mainstreamed in your room.

• Prepare an introductory letter to parents and students explaining classroom policies.

Closer to the start of actual instruction, effective classroom managers plan their lessons well enough in advance to ensure that their students remain engaged in learning. This lesson planning should be detailed in your mind if not written down. Effective teachers "walk through" their lessons in their minds before teaching them in the classroom. Teachers need to review how the lesson will begin, what type of procedure will be followed, when and how materials will be distributed, what interaction patterns will be used with students, how students will complete seatwork assignments, how corrective feedback will be given, and how an activity will end and the next begin without chaos erupting. Incorrect timing of any of the above procedures can lead to students straying from the task at hand. For example, if you pass out materials for independent work before they are to be used and then expect the students to listen to you, you will be fighting an uphill battle. This seemingly small matter can lead to big problems; unfortunately it is a common occurrence in many classrooms. Likewise, if you do not plan ahead for those students who finish their independent assignments sooner than others, you are asking for the normal flow of the lesson to be interrupted and possible problems to emerge. The following are management suggestions to consider in your preparation to teach a lesson:

• Have all materials ready to use well in advance of the actual lesson.
• Decide on how and when materials will be used.
• Know when you will distribute materials to students. Be careful not to distribute materials at the wrong time.
• When manipulatives are used in the primary grades, allow time for students to "play" with them before they can use them for the lesson's purpose.
• Plan more than one way to explain a particular concept to your students. Anticipate that some students will not understand after the first go-around.
• Think through your lesson to highlight times when students will be moving around the room. Plan ahead for smooth transitions.
• Plan how you will handle independent assignments—directions, manner of completion, collection of finished products, activities for those students who finish early—and how you intend to monitor student attention to the assignment.

Managing Group Instruction

Good classroom managers successfully orchestrate group instruction and attend to a multitude of human interactions that occur continuously throughout the day. Obviously, some teachers are more successful in managing groups of students day in and day out than others. What separates the more effective managers from the less effective? Successful classroom managers generally think ahead to avoid potential problems, sense the proper pace of a lesson, and have a continuous grasp of the total classroom situation. In addition, the work of Kounin (1970) identified several effective group techniques to ensure smooth running and productive instruction. These techniques can be planned to a certain degree, and they will help you deal effectively with group instruction. Kounin identified successful managers as possessing the following attributes: "withitness," overlapping, smoothness of transition, momentum, group alerting, and accountability. Here is what these terms mean:

- *Withitness* refers to a teacher's ability to be continuously aware of what is going on in the classroom and to communicate this awareness to students.
- *Overlapping* refers to a teacher's ability to do more than one thing at a time in the classroom without getting frustrated.
- *Smoothness of transitions* refers to the ability to go from one activity to another or one part of a lesson to another without wasting time and without undue delay.
- *Momentum* means the teacher's ability to pace lessons at a "just right" speed with few delays.
- *Group alerting* has to do with the teacher's ability to keep student attention during lessons.
- *Accountability* refers to the teacher's ability to know how well students are learning.

It does take time to develop these abilities; it does not just happen. However, you can develop these techniques: They are learned, not innate, traits. Successfully implementing these techniques relates directly to providing quality instructional time for your students. The following are management suggestions to consider while teaching a lesson:

- Remember to have the students' attention before you begin.
- Be sensitive to the correct timing of your explanation. Notice non-verbal cues from students that indicate interest or lack of interest.
- Look for indications of lack of understanding.
- Do not try to cover too much in a single lesson.
- Do not dwell too long on a topic or a response. On the other hand, do not leave a question hanging.
- Vary your questioning techniques depending on your instructional goal (see Chapter 4).
- Enforce classroom rules fairly and consistently.
- Keep interruptions to a minimum.
- Anticipate problems and handle any misbehavior quickly and in as positive a manner as possible.

- Provide feedback to students that is related to the academic task at hand.
- Circulate around the room.

Monitoring of Student Progress

Checking on how students are accomplishing instructional goals serves three purposes: 1) to tell you how well students are understanding new material, 2) to help you to focus your students' thinking on specific learnings, and 3) to serve to maintain an atmosphere conducive to learning. The effective monitoring of student progress offers a wonderful example of how management and instructional concerns are truly interdependent.

It would be ideal, of course, if students automatically mastered new learning after an initial presentation or coverage by the teacher, but in reality, students need reinforcement and at times reteaching to learn new material. Therefore, teachers must keep an eye on student progress and be able to respond quickly and appropriately. One way to do so is to monitor classroom discussion seatwork activities, group projects, and cooperative groups. Picking up on student needs at an early stage and responding effectively not only enhances student learning but prevents management problems. The specific nature of the feedback is important. A preponderance of negative feedback or of vague comments is not beneficial. As much as possible, you want to give task-related or academically focused feedback that is specific to the work at hand and redirects the student's thinking or helps to clarify a response. If a student is not completing his or her work as instructed, an example of a task-related comment would be, "John, we are working on pages 27 and 28 in your algebra book and we will go over the answers in fifteen minutes." If a student responds with an incomplete answer, a task-related comment might be, "You are on the right track, Jane, but can you tell me more regarding why the experiment did not work?" The more positive and specific the feedback is to the instructional goal and the expected response, the more students will learn, and the fewer the management problems will be.

The study of feedback that teachers provide to students, especially the use of praise, to reinforce and motivate their learning has been a topic of interest in the study of teaching (Brophy, 1981). Contrary to the popular belief that "you can't praise students enough," findings on the effectiveness of the use of praise by teachers have been mixed. Depending on the situation and the students, praise (too much or too little, or too general in nature) can negatively affect student learning. Praising one student in one way may be a positive reinforcer, but to another student that same praise might be a negative reinforcer. Try to use praise as a positive reinforcer and a vehicle to develop intrinsic student motivation. The following are management suggestions to consider in monitoring student progress:

- Have students show their work to you.
- Have students demonstrate the particular skill or knowledge.
- Ask students directly how they are proceeding with the activity.
- Provide meaningful feedback.

- Monitor independent activities by walking around the room and stopping to work with individual students on the assignment. Give immediate feedback.
- Give explicit direction for the task or assignment. Go over the first two or three examples to be certain the students understand the task.
- Make expectations clear.
- Plan a variety of activities and assignments.
- Check for student understanding before going on to the next major point.
- Have students work in teams of three or four and circulate among the teams to check progress.
- Be sensitive to signs of confusion—unnecessary movement or talking, puzzlement, lack of correct response to an easy question.
- Return student assignments with written feedback as quickly as possible.
- Have parents initial completed homework assignments.
- Be available to help students and to give positive feedback.
- Make sure assignments make sense to students. Ask them to state the purpose of the assignment.

Different Contexts

If the learning goal is student mastery of basic skills and knowledge, the effective manager takes direct control of the learning. The teacher formally explains what is to be learned in a group setting, keeps students working on academic activities by limiting discussion and student input, communicates directly and indicates an awareness of what is going on, monitors student progress, and controls the pacing of the lesson. Though this sounds old-fashioned and controlling, this "control" is maintained in a supportive atmosphere conducive to learning. Also, the effective manager is goal-driven. The controlling nature of this scenario is necessary to assure that available time for instruction is used properly. The major difference between this type of control and the use of negative reinforcers, of course, is that the atmosphere created by the teacher is pervasively positive. If you manage your class effectively but do so by using negative reinforcers, achievement can be adversely affected.

It is important to note that this style of management works best for teaching basic skills and knowledge in a content area. For developing inquiry and thinking skills, however, less teacher control and more student choice and input are advantageous. Again, managerial concerns depend upon a host of variables. You must exercise sound professional judgment based on your own situation and instructional goals.

To achieve your instructional goals in the most effective manner possible, teachers use a variety of grouping procedures to help students learn. Today the literature on teaching and classroom management tells us that grouping for instruction is a means to capitalize on student differences and increase student achievement (Burns, Roe, & Ross, 1996). Students learn from one another in a group, and are more likely to work productively in groups than individually. Effective teachers plan and use a variety of groupings (whole, small, partner, interest, cooperative, and research) throughout the year to fit specific tasks.

The focus on prevention rather than correction in classroom management simply makes good sense. When teachers put in the time to plan all facets of their instruction ahead of time, it is reasonable to assume their efforts will pay off in school achievement. Although some may argue that emphasizing prevention belabors the obvious, many "obvious" propositions that were accepted through the ages have been found to be false when put to empirical tests. Furthermore, the notion of preventive classroom management strategies has the advantage that it can be used by teachers immediately. Teachers have direct control over initiating preventive strategies.

Personal Characteristics of Teachers

Personal characteristics will also affect how well you fare as a classroom manager. Not every teacher will have the same personality, of course. Effective teachers certainly have different personalities. Regardless of personality type, however, success with students will be linked to your genuine appreciation of students, enjoying the teaching/learning process, treating students equitably and with respect, allowing students to feel at home and valued in the classroom, and communicating concern for them. Successful teachers know their students, both personally and academically, and communicate this interest to them. They "create" a community of learners. Students should never feel they are merely computer identification numbers. Teachers who take the time to know their students are practicing preventive classroom management and will be successful in their classroom teaching.

Stopping Misbehavior

Even in the best of classrooms, management problems still occur that require intervention by the teacher. The level of response can be viewed from a nonverbal response to a simple reprimand to removal of a student(s) from the classroom (see Figure 5.1). There is no sure formula for handling management or discipline problems once they surface in the classroom. Knowing several possible means of dealing with student misconduct, however, will help you respond properly. Your response to a disturbance will depend upon your ability to prioritize the severity of the problem.

During a lesson, your goal should be to develop a low-key style that will keep students working on their assignments. Losing your cool or giving an extremely negative response will probably undo any good previously accomplished. In addition, these actions have a widespread effect on other members of the class. This effect has been called the "ripple effect" by Kounin. He labels a teacher's responses to misbehavior as "desists." The use

Low	*Moderate*	*High*
Silence. "Evil eye," icy stare. Physical proximity—move toward disruptive student while continuing with lesson. Praise acceptable behavior of other students. Remind students of your expectation for them in the activity at hand. Remove materials a student is using for a short period of time.	Change tone of voice. Isolate student from group for a short period of time. Direct a task-related comment to the student(s). Remind students of certain class rules and procedures. Walk over to student and quietly tell him/her that type of behavior is unacceptable and that working on assigned material is what should be done. Direct a question to student regarding activity. Take away student privileges. Discuss problem with group. Individually remind student that learning is his/her responsibility—not yours. Contact parents. Write up a contract and have student sign it.	Firmly inform student(s) of consequences of the action. Give ten seconds for student(s) to stop. Send for help if there is potential for physical violence. Keep other students away from disruptive student(s). Remove student from class. Review incident with class and remind students of classroom rules and procedures.

FIGURE 5.1   *Response to Classroom Disruptions*

of negative desists or responses to misbehavior is especially counterproductive to a positive social and academic climate in the classroom. Desists that clearly identify the student, clearly communicate that the behavior is unacceptable, and clearly give the reason for the behavior being unacceptable are more effective than general reprimands.

Tied to prevention of management problems and handling of discipline problems is keeping lines of communication open with parents. There is also a ripple effect that goes on when contacting parents concerning a student's progress or lack of progress. Class rules and procedures should be clearly communicated to parents both in writing and in person. Nothing helps build rapport with parents more than open communication, beginning from day one. In the event of an embarrassing situation or a discipline problem, it is essential that you inform parents. A crisis or potential problem is more easily solved if you have had previous positive communication with the parents. To reflect on different types of classroom management problems and possible solutions, you are encouraged to complete Pause and Reflect: Self-Monitoring Activity 5.1 (p. 73).

Conflict Resolution

Conflict with students and between students are inevitable in the classroom. The manner in which you handle such conflicts will have direct effects on not only the students involved and yourself but also the attitudes of other students in the class. Additionally, your ability to handle conflicts productively will go a long way toward maintaining a positive classroom climate and ultimately fostering student achievement. There is not just one strategy or tactic to resolve a conflict. There are several options available to you, including withdrawing, forcing, smoothing, compromising, and confronting (Johnson, 1990). Each strategy should be utilized at different times depending upon the situation. While emphasizing that all five strategies need to be used depending on the conflict, Johnson states:

> In most conflicts, you will want to confront and smooth, since these are the two most effective strategies. When the goal is important, confront, and when the goal is unimportant to you, smooth. Both of these strategies maintain good relationships. Compromising is usually only a good idea if you have limited time and cannot negotiate a mutually satisfying solution to the conflict (p. 249).

The basis for successful conflict resolution through confrontation is communication with the student(s). The following are the steps to follow when you decide to confront the student and negotiate a resolution to a conflict:

1. Confront the opposition.
2. Jointly define the conflict.
3. Communicate any changes of positions and feelings.
4. Communicate cooperative intentions.
5. Take the other person's perspective accurately and fully.
6. Coordinate your motivation and the other's to negotiate in good faith.
7. Reach an agreement (Johnson, 1990, p. 238).

The keys to effective intervention are first and foremost teaching conflict resolution to students and then keeping your cool, communicating collaboratively with students, avoiding extremely negative responses, responding (as the situation warrants) as quickly as possible, and being unafraid to ask for help from other professionals. Every teacher will have discipline problems, and you should realize that you are not expected to solve all problems by yourself. You are a member of a team that may include your principal, curriculum supervisor, social worker, guidance counselor, specialized teachers (reading, speech, special education), fellow classroom teachers, and parents. Do not be afraid to consult these people to help in correcting a problem.

Pause and Reflect : Self-Monitoring Activity 5.1

Classroom Management Problems and Solutions

There are many effective techniques to handle a particular problem. List below the problem and the techniques employed to solve it. For example:

Problem: A student in the back of the room is talking.
Solution: The teacher walkes to the back of the room, stands there for a few minutes, and continues the class discussion.

Observe or discuss classroom management problems and solutions with other students, supervising teacher, or university supervisor.

Problem:

Solution:

Problem:

Solution:

Problem:

Solution:

Thinking Like a Teacher: Recap of Major Ideas

- Teachers need to be culturally sensitive in developing their classroom management philosophy.

- Creating and maintaining an atmosphere conducive to learning require teachers to practice "preventive" classroom management techniques.

- Three key elements in achieving the goal of effective classroom management are:

    Planning of activities—long- and short-term thinking regarding the classroom environment, materials, instructional goals, and students.

    Managing group instruction—thinking ahead regarding ways to ensure smoothly flowing lessons (Kounin's techniques of withitness, overlapping, smoothness of transitions, momentum, group alerting, and accountability).

    Monitoring student progress—systematically checking student progress in fulfillment of instructional goals.

- All teachers have to deal with student misbehavior.

- Your response to a classroom disturbance will depend upon your ability to prioritize the severity of the problem and to use as low-key a response as possible to manage the conflict.

- Conflict resolution strategies include your ability to withdraw, force, smooth, compromise, or confront depending on the situation.

Chapter SIX

Culturally Responsive Pedagogy

Issues of Culture and Instruction

Diversity is a wonderful gift to our society, but often it is an unrecognized gift—at times easily discarded or even scorned. In the United States, as in other complex societies, there is a dominant or mainstream culture and perceived subordinate or nonmainstream cultures. The dominant or mainstream culture is the culture of power and largely controls the society. The perceived subordinate or nonmainstream cultures are the diverse groups that have less power and control fewer resources. It has always been the challenge of humankind to get along cooperatively and peacefully. That challenge remains substantive and grows daily as we become more interdependent as a nation. Educating all of our children, mainstream as well as nonmainstream, to meet our highest expectations is possible. However, like the fear of diversity, ignorance of how to meet the challenge is no excuse. Teachers can act as mediators (Banks, 1988) to assist students of diverse backgrounds to build upon their cultures for the development of proficiency in literacy and other academic areas, as well as the interpersonal skills required to acquire achievement in school and other mainstream settings. It is common for education majors to focus on classroom management, information giving, school routine, and daily survival to the exclusion of fresh and careful reflection on the daily life, values, history, and aspirations of the school community. Yet, today's teachers must be students of human behavior, social events and their causes, and the characteristics of the citizens they serve.

Traditionally, models of instruction have focused on single "correct" answers. These models are likely to reflect the values, ideals, and experiences of the mainstream. Within these models of instruction, biases that exclude values, ideas, and experiences of students from diverse backgrounds are prevalent. Hence, there is a lack of culturally responsive pedagogy. Another example of this traditional pattern is having students complete assignments individually, without helping one another. If students need help, they are expected to turn to the teacher, not to another student. Students who seek help from others are judged to be cheating. The teacher may see students' efforts to help one another as disruptive and disobedient, or even dishonest. Students from diverse culture groups in turn may think it unfair and unreasonable for the teacher not to allow them to help one another. Fortunately, this mismatch can be overcome if teachers build opportunities for the learners to work together into many classroom activities. Gradually, teachers can teach the learners to distinguish times when they are to work alone and seek help only from the teacher, and times when they may seek help from peers.

The monolithic culture transmitted by the U.S. schools in the form of pedagogy, curricula, instruction, classroom configuration, and language (Walker, 1987) dramatizes the lack of fit and imbalance of power between the mainstream and the nonmainstream experiences. Most educators do not intend to discriminate against students, but discrimination results when old patterns are perpetuated. Teachers may unconsciously select for success only those children who are from mainstream backgrounds similar to their own (Spindler & Spindler, 1990). Describing groups as subordinate or dominant emphasizes the idea that inequality in educational outcomes is rooted in the power relationships among groups (McLaren, 1989; Ogbu, 1987). If all instruction could be the same for all students in each grade, teaching would be easy. The complexity of teaching is quickly realized, however, when one tries to differentiate one's instruction according to student needs and the content to be taught.

The problem of bridging the school and the home is a critical one. Students of diverse backgrounds should not be forced to choose between being successful in school and being true to their own cultural identities. The problem is compounded in urban schools where students come from many different groups and speak many different languages. Culturally responsive pedagogy in this instance involves more than matching instruction to cultural features. Instead, it is a matter of adjusting and adapting instruction to meet the needs of all students. Dwyer (1991) identifies four domains of instruction at which "good" teachers excel: 1) content knowledge, 2) teaching for student learning, 3) creating a classroom community for student learning, and 4) teacher professionalism. These are traditional ideals that are taught in institutions of teacher preparation. Villegas (1991) has extended these four domains for teachers who serve a student population that is culturally and linguistically diverse. She suggests that "good" teachers in these classroom contexts incorporate culturally responsive pedagogy, meaning that they adjust their teaching strategies in response to the learning styles, values, beliefs, and experiences of their students. As each adjustment is made, the teacher weighs its effectiveness and decides if further adjustments are needed. For example, do not assume that all Native Americans are just like the mainstream. At the same time, recognize that many Native Americans are people of two cultures, and they may lead mainstream lifestyles. If you are alert, sensitive, and active in your setting, you will meet Native Americans representing all positions on a mainstream to nonmainstream cultural continuum. Think about their roots and goals. Consider the events and conditions that are important to them. Respect those things and work to incorporate community values, skills, knowledge, and aspirations into your classroom. This perspective allows all students to be successful both in their relationship to the mainstream and in their relationship to their own communities.

Types of Learnings

As you begin to observe and teach individual and integrated lessons, you will find that some learning outcomes are specific or direct and some are open-ended or indirect. Basically, content areas and important skills within each area involve two broad types of learnings: direct and inquiry. What we call direct learning lessons are sometimes referred to as explicit, systematic, or structured, depending on the author. This traditional type of learning is amenable to specific learning objectives in which observable student behavior can be verified using criterion-referenced or standardized tests. It is further characterized by acquiring knowledge, scope and sequence, measuring aptitude, the textbook as the primary source, assessment as an event, learning in separate disciplines, and different standards for different students.

Inquiry learning lessons, with a more constructionist approach, lend themselves to performance-based and informal, alternative assessments. Embedded in this approach to education is the understanding that language and culture, and the values that accompany them, are constructed in both home and community environments (Cummins, 1986; Heath, 1981). It acknowledges that learners come to school with some constructed knowledge about many things (Goodman, 1980) and points out that their development and learning is best understood as the interaction of past and present cognitive construction (Trueba, 1988). This learning type eliminates the lack of opportunity to engage in developmentally and culturally appropriate learning in ways other than by teacher-lead or direct learnings. Researchers describe it as a pedagogy of empowerment (Cummins, 1986), as a cultural view of providing instructional assistance and guidance (Tharp & Gallimore, 1988), or as culturally responsive pedagogy. This type of learning is characterized by using knowledge, revisiting skills and concepts at a higher/more complex level, assessing performance, use of many resources, assessment as a "dip stick" at given intervals, learning across disciplines, and high standards for all students.

Critical to the success of such practices is a responsive pedagogy for academic learning that requires a redefinition of the teacher's role. You would do well to become familiar with the cognitive, social, and cultural dimensions of learning. You must further recognize the ways in which instructional assessment and evaluation practices affect learning. Specially, you will need to be alert to the configuration of the classroom environment and the ways students interact with one another and with teachers. This will require allowing students to display their knowledge in ways that suggest their competence as learners and language users. For example, teaching in a direct approach that is exclusively for students to pass a basic skills test may result in improved test scores; if you do so, however, the students from diverse backgrounds will probably be unable to respond to critical-thinking questions. In the opposite regard, relying only on higher-level thinking will not produce the intended benefits if students are not in command of the facts that they need for this type of thinking.

In another example, through the use of a social studies curriculum that drew on students' background experiences, teachers discovered that students responded well to inquiry learning activities.

> In one fourth-grade class, . . . students continued their study of communities by researching local institutions and interviewing community members outside of class, later constructing a floor sized replica of Rough Rock complete with personalized family vehicles, homes, and livestock. Individually and in groups, they wrote and discussed personal experience stories about the project and their community. This study, the teacher noted, created high levels of interest and involvement "because I'm interacting with them, and they're not just reading someone else's idea of a community in a book." Moreover, she observed, students' expressiveness in these activities and their willingness to pose and respond to questions transferred to their work in other content areas (McCarty, Lynch, Wallace, & Bennally, 1991, p. 49).

The final analysis of this perspective is that the approaches used to show that educators are in tune with the needs of diverse students include being receptive to students, open to change, and willing to give priority to learning rather than to traditional procedures of instruction.

Direct Learnings

From research on teaching there has emerged a set of procedures that are effective in teaching a body of knowledge to students. Of course, you will need to modify any set of procedures according to your students, their grade and age, their readiness for a particular skill, and the subject. Acknowledging this limitation, however, does not diminish the importance of the six instructional functions delineated by Rosenshine and Stevens (1995) (see Figure 6.1). Teachers who use these procedures consistently produce higher-than-average achievement in their classes. Obviously, a lesson will not contain each aspect of all functions as listed. Rather, the lesson

---

1. **Review**
   Review homework.
   Review relevant previous learning.
   Review prerequisite skills and knowledge for the lesson.

2. **Presentation**
   State lesson goals, provide outline or graphic organizer.
   Present new material in small steps.
   Model procedures.
   Provide positive and negative examples.
   Use clear language.
   Check for student understanding.
   Avoid digressions.

3. **Guided Practice**
   Spend more time on guided practice.
   High frequency of questions.
   All students respond and receive feedback.
   High success rate.
   Continue practice until students are fluent.

4. **Corrections and Feedback**
   Provide process feedback when answers are correct but hesitant.
   Provide sustaining feedback, clues, or reteaching when answers are incorrect.
   Reteach material when necessary.

5. **Independent Practice**
   Students receive overview and/or help during initial steps.
   Practice continues until students are automatic (where relevant).
   Teacher provides active supervision (where possible).
   Routines are used to provide help for slower students.

6. **Weekly and Monthly Reviews**

FIGURE 6.1   Functions for Teaching Well-Structured Tasks

From "Advances in Research on Instruction," by B. Rosenshine, May/June 1995, *Journal of Educational Research*, 88(5). Reprinted with permission.

should employ each function to the degree that the students' abilities and needs demand at a given time. It is important to reiterate that these teaching procedures have been found effective in teaching systematic, direct, or structured knowledge and skills in school subjects; that is, in direct instruction. At the heart of this process is the direct explanation and demonstration of a given skill by the teacher. Direct learnings can be broken down into a series of parts. The teacher explains the task at hand in small steps using examples and counterexamples. This can be accomplished through the inductive or discovery process or the deductive process. In the inductive process the teacher leads the students to discover the skill by questioning them using examples and counterexamples. The deductive process begins with the teacher telling the students what the knowledge or skill is and then using examples to support the definition. Both the inductive and deductive methods of explaining new knowledge and skills are effective; the choice of one over the other is a matter of style, taking into consideration the learning objective and students. The second major part of this process is teacher-supervised practice. Succinctly, this means that the teacher completes a few problems or examples with the students to make sure they understood the teacher's initial explanations. This is followed by independent practice to ensure that the students master the particular skill. The key to this process is student involvement with the teacher. Teachers who command the attention of their students while teaching direct learnings are more likely to have students learn than those who do not. This direct instruction procedure promotes the productive use of classroom time and student learning.

Inquiry Learnings

Teaching does not just involve ensuring that students can adequately handle structure or explicit knowledge in a particular subject area. Clearly these learnings are important and are assessed on basic skill tests and various standardized tests. Effective teaching also involves teaching students to think critically and creatively. This requires a different style of teaching from that used for direct learning. Both styles are absolutely necessary. Addressing this issue, Rosenshine and Stevens (1986) state

> These explicit teaching procedures are most applicable in those areas where the objective is to master a body of knowledge or learn a skill which can be taught in a step-by-step manner. Thus, these procedures apply to the teaching of facts that students are expected to master so that they can be used with new information in the future. Examples include arithmetic facts, decoding procedures, vocabulary, musical notation, English grammar, the factual parts of science and history, the vocabulary and grammar of foreign languages, and the factual and explicit parts of electronics, cooking, and accounting.
>
> Similarly, these procedures apply to the teaching of processes or skills that students are expected to apply to new problems or situations. This includes mathematical computation, blending sounds in decoding, map reading, the mechanics of writing personal and business letters, English grammar, applying scientific laws, solving algebraic equations, or tuning an automobile engine. In these cases, the student is taught a general rule which is then applied to new situations (p. 377).

The authors also state that these procedures are "least applicable for teaching in areas which are 'ill-structured,' that is, where the skills to be taught do not follow explicit steps . . . teaching composition and writing of term papers, analyses of literature, problem solving in specific content areas, discussion of social issues, or the development of unique or creative responses" (p. 377). Unfortunately, the literature on teaching has concentrated on the teaching of specific content and skills assessable on tests (direct learnings). Some concurrence is beginning to emerge, however, on the indicators of effective teaching of inquiry objectives. Student learning of critical and creative processes tends to be successful when the classroom teacher sets aside time for students to engage in thinking activities. The message is clear: If students are not asked to think, they will not do so. The simple matter of allocated time is vital to developing inquiry abilities. With the pressure to have students pass state-mandated literacy exams, many teachers do not allot time for any objectives other than those assessed on the state exams. Most of the learning assessed on these exams is systematic or direct in nature. Thus, students are not given the opportunity to think on higher levels. The current definition of basic skills unfortunately does not include the ability to think on higher levels. Both types of learning are "basic skills," and both should receive adequate attention in our schools. Also, each type of learning contributes strongly to the other. A literate person possesses both facts and understandings and is able to use information to analyze and think divergently. A good thing to realize is that you will have control over whether you allocate time for inquiry activities; that is, over whether you allow students to think or not. In a classic text on teaching thinking skills by Raths et al. (1966, 1986), the authors postulate a positive relationship between an emphasis on thinking skills in the classroom and student behavior. The text is a helpful source for numerous practical activities that teachers can use to develop thinking skills at all grade levels and in every subject.

Is mere exposure to thinking activities enough to foster higher-level thinking? It may be to a small degree, but students must be given an explanation of the inquiry skill and guidance in its development. This "direct explanation," however, is different in nature from the direct instruction model. It is important to remember that the initial learning of a particular inquiry skill (e.g., how to judge reasonableness and relevancy of information or how to go about planning a trip to Egypt) will require an explanation of that skill. It is the practice (both supervised and independent), however, that is treated differently. The underlying difference is in pacing and control. In the teaching of a direct or explicit learning objective the teacher transmits knowledge to students in a didactic or formal manner. In teaching an inquiry goal, the teacher acts as a facilitator, building on students' existing knowledge and guiding learning. Even so, the teacher must communicate the purpose of the inquiry skill and its relevance to students, bring prior experiences to bear on the current issue, use clear and relevant examples in discussing the process, provide occasional summaries of main points, use task-related comments and probing questions to clarify points, involve as many students as possible in discussions, and be ready to reteach or offer alternative explanations depending on student understanding. However, the time given to independent learning of an inquiry ability is more extensive, and greater student interaction is recommended. Different grouping procedures (e.g., research, interest, partner, cooperative) can be used to a greater degree to allow students the opportunity to collect data on a topic, analyze and synthesize the information, and react to and report their findings. To help reflect on different types of learnings, you are encouraged to complete number two of Pause and Reflect: Self-Monitoring Activity 6.1 (p. 85). Figure 6.2 summarizes the major differences between direct and inquiry instruction.

Complex Instruction and Inquiry Learning

Instruction is complex when a variety of grouping patterns and materials are in simultaneous use in the classroom. Complex instruction, initiated in 1978 at the Stanford University School of Education with Dr. Elizabeth Cohen, is suitable for classrooms with minority, low-income, and language-different students as well as other settings that feature learners with a wide range of academic skills. Special attention is given to the creation of equity in the context of intellectually challenging curricular materials and the use of small problem-solving groups.

Complex instruction models the real work of scientific investigations within the classroom. Students work in small groups on open-ended, uncertain tasks requiring multiple intellectual abilities. Teachers of complex instruction use classroom management strategies that enable students to use each other as resources. Specific treatments raise the expectations for competence of low-status students. Complex instruction is a tool that helps teachers reach a wide variety of students using inquiry-based curricula. The use of cooperative norms and student roles allow students to successfully exercise authority when it is delegated to them. In all subject areas, the most fundamental learning among students in a complex instruction classroom is thinking skills.

The types of learnings that occur in complex instruction include 1. factual content relevant to the topic unit; 2. generalizable intellectual processes such as how to measure, how to conduct a systematic inquiry, and how to keep accurate records; 3. generalizable concepts and principles such as the idea of a system, stratification as a principle of social organization, and the complex relationship between area and perimeter; 4. social skills, which contribute to the successful conduct of intellectual inquiry in a group setting; and 5. communication skills, which involve an increased sophistication in the use of language, both oral and written. This approach of inquiry learning is different from the direct learning methods that emphasize learning labels. In contrast, it requires active involvement of the learner in organizing and applying intellectual skills toward ends.

One critical feature of intellectual functioning is the ability to combine concepts and skills into strategies for solving problems. Learning to develop these kinds of strategies involves learning to become systematic and to make plans in approaching problems. Thus, the tasks students are given in complex instruction are by design open-ended, with no one right or wrong

Direct = *   Inquiry = χ

Teacher Control of the Class

No Control   Firm

			χ		*	
1	2	3	4	5	6	7

Who Directs the Learning?

Teacher   Students

*				χ		
1	2	3	4	5	6	7

Amount of Student Movement in Class

None   Much

	*				χ	
1	2	3	4	5	6	7

Social Interaction

None   Much

	*				χ	
1	2	3	4	5	6	7

Who Controls the Pacing of Instruction?

Teacher   Students

*					χ	
1	2	3	4	5	6	7

Noise in the Classroom

Very Noisy   Silence

			χ		*	
1	2	3	4	5	6	7

Who Decides What the Instructional Activities Will Be?

Teacher   Students

*			χ			
1	2	3	4	5	6	7

Amount of Independent Practice

None   Much

		*			χ	
1	2	3	4	5	6	7

Monitoring of Student Progress

None   Much

			χ			*
1	2	3	4	5	6	7

Level of Comprehension Questions

Exclusively   Exclusively
Factual   Critical

	*			χ		
1	2	3	4	5	6	7

FIGURE 6.2   Direct versus Inquiry Instruction

Pause and Reflect: Self-Monitoring Activity 6.1

Monitoring Discourse Interactions

1. What patterns of social interactions do you expect to encounter in your own educational experiences? Think back over your past and present classroom experiences as a learner. Would you characterize your interactions as mainly teacher-student or student-student? Has this pattern of interaction shaped how and what you learn? In what way?

2. Describe the approaches used by a teacher who uses direct learnings and a teacher who uses inquiry learnings. Explain how these approaches differ. Have you had both types of teachers in your student career? Select two teachers who adopted contrasting approaches and describe your experience as a learner with each one. Remember to consider teachers you may have had outside the formal school environment, such as music or art instructors and sports coaches.

answer, and offer the possibility of different routes for arriving at different solutions. Finally, it is important to talk about the strategies they develop and use. This will enable them to evaluate the effectiveness of their strategies and to examine alternative approaches. Learners have the opportunity to learn from each other and they share differing approaches to each experience (DeAvila, 1986; Cohen, 1984; Gardner, 1983; Sternberg, 1983).

Teaching a Lesson

The basic component of a direct learning lesson is the ability to show students how to do something new. The teacher transmits knowledge to students through modeling and step-by-step instructions. Upon this foundation, teachers can design a series of lessons to attain instructional goals. The components of the lesson will be based on our knowledge of the students' readiness for learning and the knowledge we have accumulated about how to learn a new skill or ability. While teaching a lesson yourself, you are encouraged to have your cooperating teacher or another student teacher complete the lesson observation report contained in Pause and Reflect: Self-Monitoring Activity 6.2 (pp. 89–90). A basic component of teaching is the ability to show students how to do something new. A plan for teaching a lesson is given below, with a brief explanation of each component. The suggested elements of each component are just that—suggestions. Depending on the particular grade, students, and instructional goals, you can expect to modify the components to fit your situation. The components in teaching a direct lesson follow:

1. Major activity
2. Instructional goal(s)
3. Materials/Supplies
4. Focus activity (build on prior knowledge to prepare to learn)
5. Teaching (procedures: Define [examples and nonexamples] or explore for concept development, model or inquiry, scaffold with supervised practice or cooperative group interaction, and independent practice or conclusion)
6. Evaluation (student and teacher), follow-up activity, extension or reteach

Major Activity

To help create a proper mind-set for teaching a new skill or ability, it is recommended that you first list the major activities. Following are some examples:

Writing a character sketch
Auditory discrimination of vowel sounds
Use of the newspaper
Estimating with multiples of 10

Writing editorials

Short stories

Comparing fractional numbers

Punctuation marks

Exponential and logarithmic functions

Directed reading activity (using a basal reader)

Declension of irregular adjectives

Improvement of study skills

Summarizing *The Merchant of Venice*

Instructional Objective(s)

Using the major activity you have chosen, you should state the goal of the lesson. This statement should explain exactly what you expect students to know or be able to do as a result of the lesson. If the lesson has a direct learning objective, the goal should be pinpointed with specificity, with the goal specified in terms of observable student behavior and a specified competency level. If the lesson has an inquiry objective, less specificity is required and the intended goal should reflect diagnostic information on students. Regardless of the grade and subject area, you should be teaching what the students need to know. This can be accomplished only by knowing the instructional needs of your students. Also implicit in stating the instructional goal is your awareness of the prerequisite skills and knowledge that the students must possess to be successful in the lesson. Acquiring the habit of identifying prerequisite skills and knowledge will greatly enhance student learning. You will be confident in evaluating student learning in a particular lesson knowing students do not lack the prerequisite skills and knowledge.

Materials and Supplies

Listing the materials to be used in the lesson is an absolute necessity for teachers-in-training. While this component may seem mundane, it is important. The materials you select should be on the proper level of difficulty to help ensure student involvement. Knowing what materials you will be using and having them prepared before the class begins is a problem for some teachers-in-preparation. As you can anticipate, if materials are not ready to use, you may lose some or all control of the class. Management problems can follow; worst of all, you may be unable to realize the instructional goal.

Focus Activity

This component highlights the beginning of your lesson. By "focus activity" we mean attempting to enlist interest in the topic of the lesson. Developing background for the lesson entails reviewing past learnings related to the new information and concepts to be presented in the lesson to help make the lesson relevant to students. There are numerous ways to motivate and

Pause and Reflect: Self-Monitoring Activity 6.2

Lesson Evaluation Report

Ask another student teacher or your cooperating teacher to observe and complete a lesson evaluation on a lesson you teach (see the Lesson Evaluation form below). Record the absence or presence of each lesson component, and write as many comments as time allows. If one of the questions below is not appropriate to the lesson, write *NA* (not applicable) after the question. An alternative to monitoring a whole lesson would be to concentrate on one specific aspect of a lesson.

Lesson Evaluation

Observation Report

Lesson Objective: _____ Direct or Inquiry Learning? _____

Yes	No		*Comments*
		1. Motivation and Background	
_____	_____	Was background information given?	_____
_____	_____	Was the goal of the lesson communicated to the students?	_____
_____	_____	Was a purpose established for completing the lesson?	_____
_____	_____	Were students motivated to take an interest from the beginning?	_____
		2. Teaching	
_____	_____	Was the objective explained adequately?	_____
_____	_____	Were sufficient examples and illustrations given?	_____
_____	_____	Were the teaching materials adapted to the students' needs?	_____
_____	_____	Was a sufficient variety of activities used?	_____
_____	_____	Were occasional summaries provided by the teacher?	_____
_____	_____	Was progress assessed and rewarded?	_____
_____	_____	Were all students involved in the lesson?	_____
_____	_____	Was the teacher sensitive to wait-time?	_____
_____	_____	Were task-related comments and probing questions used?	_____

Continued

Lesson Evaluation (Continued)

Yes	No		Comments
		3. Supervised Practice	
_____	_____	Did the teacher go over a few examples with the students?	_____
_____	_____	Was any reteaching necessary?	_____
_____	_____	Did the teacher summarize important points?	_____
		4. Independent Practice	
_____	_____	Was the practice understood by the students?	_____
_____	_____	Was enough time allocated for students to complete the practice?	_____
_____	_____	Was there enough practice for students to master the intended goal?	_____
_____	_____	Did the teacher monitor the practice?	_____
_____	_____	Did the teacher recap main points?	_____
		5. Evaluation	
_____	_____	Did the teacher evaluate the intended goal?	_____
_____	_____	Did the students seem satisfied with the lesson?	_____

to provide background for lessons, and following are some ideas that may prove useful:

Use illustrations in the text to develop interest.

Have students discuss a personal experience related to the major activity of the lesson.

Use direct experiences. Bring in real objects, make trips outside the class, invite in a guest lecturer, perform an experiment.

Discuss new concepts to avoid misconceptions.

Use the arts. Listen to music or display pieces of art.

By motivating and developing background you will be helping students create a mind-set for the material to follow. Time spent in this readiness phase will help students "tune in" to the lesson and help maintain their attention and concentration. This part of the lesson provides students with a purpose for learning. This purpose should be specific and it should relate to subsequent learning. Making sure students know the purpose of the lesson also helps keep their attention and improve their understanding.

Teaching

The heart of the lesson is teaching—the manner in which you explain, inform, or demonstrate what you want students to know. This can be done inductively; that is, with a step-by-step explanation, proceeding from the simple to the complex, and using examples and illustrations that lead students to a generalization. It may also be done deductively, first telling students the generalization and then supplying examples to verify it. Where possible, concrete examples should be used to break down the new material into meaningful units. You should carefully plan classroom questions on an appropriate level of difficulty and at different levels of intellectual thought to determine student understanding and clarify difficult points. Also, sufficient time should be allowed after posing a question before you respond to a student. Many students need time (at least three seconds) to process the question and formulate an answer. Your sensitivity to "wait-time" (Rowe, 1974) will help increase classroom interaction and student learning. In addition, to check on student understanding and maintain student attention you should give specific verbal feedback with task-related comments and probing questions (see the Planning for Classroom Discussion section later in this chapter for further explanation). You should always be ready to modify teaching procedures and materials based on the students' responses. If the students are encountering little difficulty, you should increase the pace of the lesson so that you do not lose them. If students are encountering difficulty, you may have to slow down and reteach the instructional goal in another fashion. Providing occasional restatements and summarizing main ideas are ways to develop and reaffirm intended goals. It is important for you to discover the degree to which the students are catching on and to give them the necessary feedback so that they know what needs improvement.

Supervised Practice

Before allowing students to complete an independent assignment, it is important that you "walk" students through a few examples or through part of an independent activity and summarize key points. This will let you know if the students have understood your initial explanation and have begun to transfer this learning to a new situation.

Independent Practice

Meaningful practice should be provided to ensure transfer of a new skill or ability to a variety of situations. It is important to make sure that independent assignments are understandable to students. Depending on the instructional goal, you should still monitor such practice indirectly. In the case of direct instruction, even independent practice should be monitored because more teacher involvement will mean more student learning. The independent practice should be on an appropriate level of difficulty to ensure a high success rate, and the practice should be plentiful enough for mastery and transfer of the new skill. Without practice to the point of over-learning and automaticity (application of the skill without thinking about it), students are likely to accumulate "half-learnings." In the case of inquiry instruction, teacher behavior is quite different. Instead of directing independent practice, you assume the role of a facilitator. There should be little concern for moving the practice along at a rapid pace, since the students should control the pacing of activities, the amount of interaction, and the instructional activities themselves. Regardless of the type of instructional goal, it is important that you recap the main points of the lesson at the end of the activity.

Evaluation and Follow-Up

Evaluating a lesson to see if you achieved the prestated goal can be accomplished in a number of ways; for example, by using a worksheet, test, discussion, teacher-made or commercial game, or group activity. Evaluation is a process that should pervade each instructional lesson. Your monitoring and evaluating of student progress should be included in each part of your lesson. By doing so, student time-on-task will be increased throughout the lesson and final student achievement of the instructional goal will be realized. Whatever materials are used to evaluate whether the lesson's goal was achieved, you should check to make sure the evaluation reflects the instructional goal and content of the lesson. If students perform well, you can feel reasonably sure that your teaching was appropriate and your students are ready for the next step. If students did not achieve the objective of the lesson, it is necessary for you to reexamine your teaching procedures and decide how to reteach the original learning objective. This final lesson evaluation is the best feedback for both you and the students because it lets you know how to teach tomorrow's lesson. Following is a review of key lesson components:

1. Major activity
   - Instructional goal(s)
   - Materials/supplies
   - Be sure materials are ready at the start of the lesson

2. Focus activity
   - Review past learnings
   - Elicit student interest
   - Communicate purpose of lesson

3. Teaching
   - Begin lesson with students on-task
   - Present lesson inductively or deductively with many examples and illustrations
   - Be sure the level of difficulty of the presentation is appropriate so that students will be successful
   - Maintain a brisk pace
   - Give feedback with task-related comments and probing questions
   - Be sensitive to "wait-time"
   - Provide summary of main points

4. Supervised practice
   - Complete a few examples with students
   - Provide appropriate feedback
   - Summarize key points

5. Independent practice
   - Make sure independent assignments are clear
   - Make sure material is at an appropriate level of difficulty to ensure a high success rate
   - Plan sufficient time and materials to achieve automaticity
   - Monitor student practice by circulating around the room
   - Recap main points

6. Evaluation

Meeting Needs in the Multicultural Classroom

When teaching all students, consideration needs to be made for cultural and language differences. Teachers must know their students' backgrounds, must employ additional knowledge and skills in their teaching, and must use specialized techniques and guidelines in making instructional decisions in the classroom. Students will differ in terms of values, learning styles, communication patterns, and orientation to schooling, to name a few. These differences not only affect how well students will learn but also should indicate differences in how they should be taught.

From a study of cultural differences and learning styles (Golnick & Chinn, 1986), many culturally and linguistically diverse students have a relational and field-dependent learning style. These students may function better in cooperative, informal, and person-oriented structured environments with teachers and students working together for a common goal. A style of careful guidance and facilitation by teachers rather than tight controlling of student learning is preferred. In discussing the effects of cultural background on learning, Coballes-Vega (1992) states:

> For some African American, Native American, and Hispanic students, cooperative grouping instructional activities may be better because they parallel the context for learning found in their cultures. Teachers can consider modifying traditional direct instruction to include other types of instruction from which all students can benefit.

There are a number of dialects in the English language. According to Harris and Hodges (1995), a dialect is "a variety of the language of a speech community differing enough from other varieties of that language in pronunciation, grammar, and vocabulary to be considered a distinct type, but not a separate language because there is mutual understandability" (p. 87). Although standard English is most common in our country, there are dozens of dialects and it is important to realize that none is superior to the others and that each is logical and governed by a set of internal rules. Furthermore, a student's competence is unrelated to his or her use of dialect. It is crucial that teachers be aware of dialects and know something about any dialects spoken by the students they teach. This is important for two reasons: First, by being aware of particular phonological, syntactical, and semantic differences, teachers will not count characteristics of the dialect as errors; second, teachers can show respect for a nonstandard dialect while at the same time modeling standard English. Specific instructional guidelines to use in planning and delivering effective instruction to students who speak a nonstandard dialect are:

Recognize, accept, and value students from diverse linguistic backgrounds and their dialects.

Become familiar with the dialect and note its specific differences from standard English.

Do not penalize students for dialectal errors in reading as long as comprehension is unaffected.

Do not expect complete mastery of standard English before success is achieved in your subject.

Integrate contributions of various ethnic groups into your instruction.

Emphasize oral language and comprehension activities in your instructional planning, take extra time to discuss and elaborate on what was read with students, focus on student ideas in discussions, and participate in real conversations with your students in order to expand English proficiency and fluency.

Activate prior knowledge and develop background knowledge on topics to be read.

Select materials to read that reflect students' backgrounds and interests.

Design classroom experiences so that students can be active through cooperative grouping and peer interaction.

In many schools, a large percentage of students have a native language other than English. It is not uncommon to have students whose native language is Polish, Navajo, Vietnamese, or Spanish, to name just a few. Hispanic students constitute a majority of non-English speakers in schools in the United States. Since learning in every subject is a language process, it should be no surprise that many students whose native language is not English experience difficulties learning in English. Unlike students who speak a dialect, many of these students do not understand spoken English and know little written English. If students are orally fluent in English, the possible difficulties are not as great. To correct this language mismatch, schools sometimes employ English-as-a-Second-Language (ESL) and bilingual approaches. ESL focuses on teaching English orally to students who speak limited English. A school's ESL program is usually a pull-out (separate) class provided in addition to regular class instruction. Bilingual instruction is characterized by concurrently teaching in both the student's native language and English. Specific guidelines to use in planning and delivering instruction to students whose native language is not English are:

Recognize, accept, and value students from different cultural backgrounds and whose native language is not English.

Know the differences between standard English and the students' native languages.

Activate prior knowledge and develop background knowledge on topics to be read.

Emphasize oral language and comprehension activities to build students' listening and speaking vocabularies (the same recommendations discussed above for students who speak a dialect other than standard English). In addition, use strategies such as shared reading, semantic mapping or webbing to increase vocabulary, shared explanations of meanings of new words and ideas expressed in text, reciprocal teaching (Palinscar & Brown, 1984—a strategy that fosters an interactive dialogue with students around the strategies of predicting what the author will talk about, summarizing what was read, generating questions about what was read, and clarifying any ambiguous points), and multiple conversational opportunities to enhance both English fluency and comprehension of assignments.

Use the strategy of "think-alouds" (that is, explain to students step-by-step how you would go about completing a task or the thinking involved in solving a problem) in helping students understand and interact with written text.

Focus on the understanding of ideas, not correct pronunciation of words.

Learn how well students can read and write in their native language and whether or not students have contact with English-speaking peers after school. This information will help in planning both classroom and homework assignments.

Select materials to be read that reflect the students' background and cultural heritage.

Encourage students to be active in learning through cooperative grouping activities and by involving students in making choices in carrying out an activity.

Unit Plans

As a college student, you do not take just one or two courses each semester but usually five or six. For this, you must be mentally prepared and must plan your semester schedule for attending class, doing homework, and allocating time for relaxation. As a teacher, instead of just teaching one subject for one or two class periods, you will teach a number of subjects and skills over several weeks and you must mentally prepare a teaching plan covering several days. Depending on the subject and the level you teach, the curriculum may already be divided into meaningful units around a particular theme. As a teacher-in-training, once you have had experience teaching an individual lesson, you may be required to teach either a mini-unit (four or five sequential lessons) or a long-range unit (nine or ten sequential lessons). The core of this set of plans remains the same—the individual lesson plan. The factors to keep in mind in planning a one- or two-week unit are the same for planning your semester or year activities. Although you will probably have curriculum guides to help in decision making, the following factors should be considered:

1. What are the major activities to be used as vehicles to teach instructional goals?
2. What are your general and specific instructional goals?
3. How much time are you tentatively allotting for each major activity?
4. How will you divide the material to be covered in reasonable units and proper sequence for instruction?
5. What is the prerequisite knowledge needed by the students to be successful in the unit?
6. How might other content subjects be integrated into the units?
7. What ways can you use to help the slow starter and motivate the fast starter who soon gets bogged down?

Integrated Instructional Learning

Integrated instruction includes units of study with a range of possibilities for many meaningful purposes to learn both content and the language.

Activities and projects span the curriculum so that students can engage in systematic and reflective inquiry for a variety of topics. As students learn, teachers collaborate, respond, facilitate, and support their efforts. By the use of themes, integrated units reflect patterns of thinking, goals, and concepts common to bodies of knowledge. They link together content from many areas of the curriculum and depict the connections that exist across disciplines (Pappas, Kiefer, & Levstik, 1995). Such instructional learning techniques allow for culturally responsible pedagogy that is student-centered.

In choosing the theme, there is no one "right" way. You should choose a theme that is broad enough to incorporate many types of resources, books, and activities. However, it should not be so broad that learners lose sight of the connections that are to be explored. Some teachers like to begin to think of the theme by planning topics according to more traditional areas such as math, science, art, poetry, or writing. In fact, collaboration between teachers with different expertise and content areas can help strengthen the unit since a broad range of resources can meet the needs of diverse cultural backgrounds. As long as these categories allow for valid exploration, the ideas are worth knowing. Also, if inquiry connects concepts to mirror the learners' experiences in the real world, the use of themes can provide a central focus for linking many subject areas.

At the onset of each unit, learners can engage in several activities that could be major avenues for introducing and exploring the theme. You may begin with students' interest (to inspire, motivate, and set purposes), an artifact (to arouse curiosity and speculation), a book (to capitalize on a rich source of ideas and starting points), or drama (to establish a context for the inquiry and a need for research). The intent is to empower the learner by creating a learning environment in which content, process, and intellectual excitement are connected.

Instructional Discourse

In classrooms across the nation, teaching events are structured daily around teacher-student dialogues. Consider the following kindergarten classroom with the teacher leading a lesson for a small group (Garcia, 1992):

Teacher: Okay, María, let's see what we can figure out about the shapes of these blocks.

María: This one's yellow.

Teacher: Sí, yellow is a color, but can you tell me what shape this block is?

María: Todos son amarillos. (They are all yellow.)

Teacher: Sí, but we want to talk about shape. Tú sabes como? (You know how?)

María: (Holding up a triangle.) This one, this one, this one, es amarillo. (is yellow)

Such instructional interaction occurs repeatedly every day in classrooms. The teacher asks a question or, as in this example, requests a student response. The student replies. Finally, the teacher evaluates the student's response and may request further elaboration. On the one hand, such conversations are an instructional strategy in that they are designed to promote learning. Yet, they are structured to take advantage of natural and spontaneous interactions, free from the didactic characteristics normally associated with formal teaching. Such interactions are engaging, center on an idea or a concept, and may shift in focus as the discussion evolves. In instructional discourse, teachers and students are responsive to what others say so that each statement or contribution builds upon, challenges, or extends a previous one. Strategically, the teacher presents ideas or experiences, clarifies, and instructs when necessary but does so efficiently without wasting time or words. Such discourse is in many ways similar to interactions that take place outside of school between children and adults. These interactions appear to be very important for learning and cognitive development in general. You are encouraged to complete number one of Pause and Reflect: Self-Monitoring Activity 6.1 (p. 85) to reflect on your own interactions as a student.

As the preceding discussion suggests, a primary issue in determining the educational needs of diverse learners is understanding instructional interaction. Children from different linguistic cultures will use language in ways that reflect their different social environments. A comprehensive understanding of instructional interactions must therefore take into consideration the linguistic and cognitive attributes of that interaction. It must consider the learner's surrounding environment and pragmatics of speech.

Flexible Lesson Planning

Although planning is absolutely crucial to successful teaching, too detailed a plan or too much reliance on the plan can thwart student learning. Certainly you want to be prepared, but you must realize that students will not perform as expected 100 percent of the time. The "unexpected" or "unplanned" happens daily, and you must be able to respond properly. A few possible reasons that would warrant a change in your initial teaching plan are presented as follows:

Students exhibit greater understanding of the lesson goal than previously expected (or the reverse).

A student responds to a question with a creative or imaginative answer that in turn leads other students to relate similar concerns.

Due to a class interruption, there is not enough class time left to finish the lesson.

In such situations, you must be sensitive to students' needs and modify your lesson accordingly. Rigidly following the lesson plan with a lack of sensitivity for the needs of the students defeats the purpose of lesson planning. Lesson planning is envisioning a blueprint for the achievement of your instructional goals, and you should include a measure of flexibility in a well-conceived plan. Remember, it is one thing to write a lesson plan two or three days before the day you will teach it, but it is quite another to execute the lesson creatively with students in the classroom. Many times your best lessons will not be entirely planned, as long as you are ready to respond depending on the needs of students.

Planning for Classroom Discussion

Since the core of a lesson is the "teaching" step, in which you explain, demonstrate, and discuss new learnings with your students, it is imperative that you carefully plan class discussion. The teacher's art of questioning is one important key to lively classroom discussions and how much students learn. Your ability to ask appropriate questions will affect student motivation and participation, development of comprehension skills in the subject area, and cognitive level of class discussions. Likewise, the students' responses can reveal their attitude and interest in learning and their achievement or lack of achievement of instructional goals.

Most teachers have been exposed to Bloom's *Taxonomy of Educational Objectives* (Bloom et al., 1956). Low-level questions are usually designated as those that represent Bloom's Knowledge and Comprehension categories and some of the Application category. High-level questions usually correspond to some questions in the Application category and questions in the Analysis, Synthesis, and Evaluation categories. Essentially, low-level questions range from dealing with concrete facts (the questions who, what, where, and when) to interpreting explicitly stated information (inferential questions, sometimes represented as how and why questions). High-level questions raise that level of thinking to creative and critical applications of information. Such questions stimulate abstract thinking (questions such as "what if" or "so what—what does it mean to me?").

Another way of categorizing classroom questions is to ask whether they encourage convergent or divergent thinking. Convergent thinking corresponds to low-level questions; these are questions that have a "right" answer. On the other hand, divergent thinking corresponds to high-level questions; these questions do not have a "right" answer. A sample question for each type of thinking is given as follows:

> Convergent thinking: What was the name of the hotel manager?
>
> Divergent thinking: Why do you think the author ended the story in this way?

As you can see, the convergent question has a right answer that can be verified. The divergent question may be answered in a number of ways, and each answer would be correct.

The types of questions asked depend on the instructional goals. In general, you should strive for a balance of low-level and high-level questions. This should be the goal, even though standardized and criterion-referenced tests mostly assess convergent thinking. Since the ultimate goal is to cultivate the students' ability to think independently, providing students with an opportunity to respond to a balanced pattern of discussion questions will stimulate their thinking on all levels.

When teaching a specific skill amenable to direct instruction, you should initially plan on asking a high percentage of low-level questions. After the students have mastered the skill on a factual level, they can be asked to use this new skill in answering high-level questions. Thus, reaching the low-level objectives will give students something to think with on a higher level. If you are developing a high-level thinking ability, you should concentrate on asking "thinking" questions, which will encourage students to rearrange the factual information they have learned in abstract and creative ways.

When you are conducting a discussion with students, situations will develop in which the students must be redirected or put back on the right track. They may need a question rephrased or further elaboration, or may need to be challenged to think critically. In such cases, it is helpful to give feedback with task-related comments and probing questions. As described in Chapter 5, task-related comments are statements to students that are specific to the work at hand. These comments are not of a general nature and help focus students' thinking on the intended goal and maintain classroom control. An example would be, "Tim, your answer to the first question is correct. Now, we will all complete the next five questions by ourselves and then we will go over the answers together." Probing questions are used to redirect and refine students' responses to a question. The following are examples of probing questions:

Are you sure you meant what you said?

Can you give me another example?

What are some other alternatives?

Can you tell me more?

What assumptions are you making?

Can you explain why?

Do you agree? Disagree?

You could plan an excellent, balanced set of questions for discussion, but if you do not involve as many students as possible, the lesson will come up short. There are several methods of calling on students during class discussions. Since the literature on teaching has not conclusively shown one method to be more effective than others, it is recommended that you vary methods depending on the content, goals, and students. To find the method that works best for you and your students is the ultimate goal. The following are different methods of calling on students:

Decide which student to call on before asking a question.

Ask a question and call on a student who "wants" to answer it.

Ask a question and call on a student at random to answer it.

Phrase your question by first stating which student you want to answer the question.

To achieve the overall goal of maximizing student participation, you need to be accepting of student responses and show them (both verbally, with pleasant tone of voice and without insulting them if they answer incorrectly; and nonverbally, through facial expressions) that you respect them and their ideas. You want to communicate a nonthreatening atmosphere in which they will feel free to respond and ask questions. To develop your questioning skills and reflect upon their effects on your students, you are encouraged to complete Pause and Reflect: Self-Monitoring Activities 6.3 (pp. 103–104) and 6.4 (p. 105–106).

Self-Monitoring FYI: Suggestions for Planning Discussion

1. Write discussion questions on 3 × 5 cards until you feel adroit in this area. As you may have already discovered, it is difficult to create specific questions extemporaneously during discussion.

2. Be certain your questions follow a logical pattern.

3. Make sure the questions are logical and are easy to understand. Be ready to reword a difficult question.

4. Plan how you intend to involve as many students as possible in the discussion.

5. Try to anticipate student responses.

6. Be sensitive to students' verbal and nonverbal responses to keep the pace running smoothly.

7. For feedback, use task-related comments that are directed specifically toward students' thinking.

8. Sustain the discussion around key ideas by using probing or clarifying questions.

9. Allow students adequate time to respond to questions (wait-time).

10. Monitor the types of questions you plan on asking and those asked by referring to the chart on Bloom's taxonomy.

11. Encourage students to ask questions.

12. Circulate around the room, never remaining in one place for an entire period.

13. Plan to have students summarize new knowledge.

Thinking Like a Teacher: Recap of Major Ideas

- Culturally responsive pedagogy is instruction suited for individual student needs and reflects each student's culture and background.

- Two major types of learning are *direct* and *inquiry*.

- Direct learnings encompass knowledge of a subject that can be taught in a step-by-step fashion. The recommended approach to teach this body of knowledge is direct instruction. In direct instruction, the teacher is in control of all aspects of the lesson content—teaching, pacing, practice, etc. Students are taught a new skill or understanding through a very structured explanation and demonstration, teacher-supervised practice, and an independent practice cycle.

- Inquiry learnings, which are those learnings not amenable to behavioral objective statements, concern themselves with critical and creative abilities. Although students initially need to learn some critical thinking processes in a step-by-step manner, the recommended teaching strategy for inquiry learnings is characterized by less teacher structure and control and more student input and independence.

- Both types of learnings are important and both types of teaching strategies should be included in a teacher's repertoire.

- Both types of learnings need to be taught with relation to the learning styles of the students in the classroom. Teaching approaches, including direct instruction, should be modified to include opportunities for peer and collaborative learning and instances for real conversations between the teacher and students when teaching culturally and linguistically diverse students.

- Teachers need to plan appropriate instruction and recognize, accept, and value students who speak a nonstandard dialect and whose native language is not English.

- Planning is an essential part of effective teaching and teachers need to know the elements of successful lessons, long-range unit considerations, necessities for flexibility, and important concerns in conducting the classroom discussion phase of teaching.

Pause and Reflect: Self-Monitoring Activity 6.3

Constructing Classroom Questions

Select a story or passage that you intend to use with students. Using the figure on page 104 as a guide, construct questions for the lesson. Be sure you have at least one question representing each category of Bloom's taxonomy.

Write your questions in the space below. After each question, identify the type of thinking it is intended to foster.

Summary of Bloom's Taxonomy and Breakdown between Lower- and Higher-Level Questions

Questioning Catetory	Bloom's Category	Student Activity	Typical Stem Words
Lower Level	Knowledge	Remembering: Facts, Terms, Definitions, Concepts, Principles.	What?, List, Name, Define, Describe.
	Comprehension	Understanding the meaning of material.	Explain, Interpret, Summarize, Give examples . . . , Predict, Translate.
	Application	Selecting a concept or skill and using it to solve a problem.	Compute, Solve, Apply, Modify, Construct.
Higher Level	Analysis	Breaking material down into its parts and explaining the hierarchical relations.	How does . . . apply? Why does . . . work? How does . . . relate to . . . ? What distinctions can be made about . . . and . . . ?
	Synthesis	Producing something original after having broken the material down into its component parts.	How do the data support . . . ? How would you design an experiment which investigates . . . ? What predictions can you make based upon the data?
	Evaluation	Making a judgment based upon a pre-established set of of criteria.	What judgments can you make about . . . ? Compare and contrast . . . criteria for . . . ?

From *Effective Classroom Questioning* (p. 5), by Stephanie S. Goodwin, George W. Sharp, Edward F. Cloutier, Nancy A. Diamond, and Kathleen A. Dalgaard, n.d., Urbana-Champaign, IL: Course Development Division, Office of Instruction Resources, University of Illinois. No copyright. Reproduction permitted.

Pause and Reflect: Self-Monitoring Activity 6.4

Monitoring Classroom Questions

Assess questioning skills by taping one of your lessons or by having another person observe the lesson. Using the figure on page 106 as a guide, rate the level of thinking required for each question asked and put a check mark under the appropriate cognitive level in Bloom's taxonomy. If it is not possible to tape the lesson, ask your supervising teacher or a fellow teacher-in-training to evaluate and record the types of questions asked in a lesson.

After the lesson, tally the number of questions asked in each cognitive level. Next, respond to the following questions:

- Did you ask questions that made students think at various cognitive levels?

- What type of question did you ask the most? the least?

- Are you satisfied with the pattern of questions asked? Yes or no?

If you answered no, what will you do differently in subsequent lessons?

- Did you ask any probing questions to clarify a point or extend students' thinking?

*Summary of Bloom's Taxonomy and Breakdown between Lower-
and Higher-Level Questions*

Questioning Catetory	Bloom's Category	Student Activity	Typical Stem Words
Lower Level	Knowledge	Remembering: Facts, Terms, Definitions, Concepts, Principles.	What?, List, Name, Define, Describe.
	Comprehension	Understanding the meaning of material.	Explain, Interpret, Summarize, Give examples . . . , Predict, Translate.
	Application	Selecting a concept or	Compute, Solve,
Higher Level		skill and using it to solve a problem.	Apply, Modify, Construct.
	Analysis	Breaking material down into its parts and explaining the hierarchical relations.	How does . . . apply? Why does . . . work? How does . . . relate to . . . ? What distinctions can be made about . . . and . . . ?
	Synthesis	Producing something original after having broken the material down into its component parts.	How do the data support . . . ? How would you design an experiment which investigates . . . ? What predictions can you make based upon the data?
	Evaluation	Making a judgment based upon a pre-established set of of criteria.	What judgments can you make about . . . ? Compare and contrast . . . criteria for . . . ?

From *Effective Classroom Questioning* (p. 5), by Stephanie S. Goodwin, George W. Sharp, Edward F. Cloutier, Nancy A. Diamond, and Kathleen A. Dalgaard, n.d., Urbana-Champaign, IL: Course Development Division, Office of Instruction Resources, University of Illinois. No copyright. Reproduction permitted.

Chapter SEVEN

Quality Time

Dimensions of Time

Studies of effective teaching and effective schools have yielded two important findings regarding time: first, the amount of time that is *allocated* to instruction in a particular subject affects how much students learn; and second, *how* this allocated time is used by teachers directly relates to student achievement (Slavin, 1997). These findings reflect the two sides of time.

Allocated time refers to the time given to cover material in a course of study. Coverage entails scheduling sufficient time for both teacher and student to engage in targeted instructional goals. This aspect of time refers to quantity; that is, the amount of time designated to the use of instructional material. School districts or state education agencies usually decide how much time is to be allocated for instruction in any one area. However, teachers must use this time for instructional purposes. Although teachers do not have much influence over the amount of time allocated for instruction from an administrative scheduling standpoint, they can abuse the allocated time by not using the full amount for a particular subject. The evidence that teachers differ in the amount of time that they allot for instruction was reported in the Beginning Teacher Evaluation Study (BTES) (Fisher et al., 1978). This highly influential study showed that teachers who allocated more time than average to teaching math and reading in the elementary school produced higher-than-average student achievement. Researchers found surprising differences in the amount of time allocated for instruction. For second-grade math, the average allocated time was from twenty-five minutes to sixty minutes per day in different classes. In fifth-grade reading, the researchers found allocated time averaged from sixty to 140 minutes per day. The BTES researchers discovered equally surprising differences in the amount of time allocated for specific skills within subject areas. For example, in one fifth-grade reading class, an average of ten minutes daily was spent on instruction in reading comprehension, in contrast to another class with an average of fifty minutes per day spent on comprehension instruction.

Stallings and Mohlman (1981) provided more specific data about the use of allocated class time by secondary school teachers. The authors reported that effective teachers spend less than 15 percent of their time on classroom management and organization matters. They spent 50 percent or more on interactive instruction with students, and no more than 35 percent of their time on monitoring independent activities. Thus, for a fifty-minute class, approximately six to eight minutes were spent on management and organization matters, at least twenty-five minutes on instruction, and from fifteen to eighteen minutes on independent assignments. All of these findings reinforce the conclusion that students will not learn if they are not given the opportunity to learn. "Opportunity to learn" is perhaps the most powerful variable that accounts for how well students learn in school.

The other side of time refers to *how* the allocated time is used by teachers in the classroom. How time is used can vary greatly from classroom to classroom depending on instructional goals and teaching strategies. This aspect of time is often referred to as quality time, the time when students are actually attending to the work at hand. Fortunately, classroom teachers have direct control over this dimension of time. Other terms for quality time are "student time-on-task" or "academic engaged time." Research on teaching clearly shows that the more time students spend engaged in learning, the higher their achievement will be. You should not be surprised to realize that during many minutes of a class students will not be actively working or paying attention. The BTES researchers also found surprising differences in the average engagement rates across various classes. They observed some classes where students were engaged 50 percent of the time and others where the students' time-on-task or engagement rate was close to 90 percent.

Examining Time Allocation

How time is used in the classroom is interrelated to and interdependent on the implementation of all the other principles of instruction. The importance of time can be appreciated if one looks at the school curriculum in terms of:

1. Time emphasis for the three program components in teaching a subject area—developmental, independent, and corrective
2. Time emphasis for direct and inquiry learnings within each subject area and across interdisciplinary instruction
3. Time emphasis for small group instructional opportunities, which foster peer and collaborative learning
4. Time emphasis for discussion about what was read between the teacher and the students

In order to examine your own use of classroom time, you are encouraged to complete Pause and Reflect: Self-Monitoring Activity 7.1 (p. 111).

Program Components

All school subjects contain three components: the developmental program, the independent or recreational program, and the corrective program. Briefly, the developmental program encompasses the teaching of all the direct and inquiry learnings needed to attain understanding and appreciation of a particular subject. The recreational program denotes the time students spend practicing the knowledge and skills taught to them in the developmental program for authentic purposes. It is also the goal of the recreational program to foster a positive attitude toward the subject at hand and to expand students' interests. The corrective program of any subject area deals with additional instruction and practice opportunities for students who for some reason fail to adequately understand the skill or topic being studied. A key to the proper use of allocated time is to maintain a balance between the three major components. Ignoring one component will lead to problems in another. For example, spending 100 percent of the allocated time in U.S. history on factual content is unlikely to produce students who want to do extended reading in this subject. Time must be given to use this factual content in a variety of independent and meaningful tasks and activities. Because of the need to prepare students for basic skill tests and accountability pressures, it is not uncommon to find teachers giving a disproportionate amount of time to direct skills in the developmental phase. This is a mistake. To produce independent learners, a balanced program is necessary. Effective teachers know the components of a complete program in their subject area and plan to use a portion of the allocated time in each phase. This does not mean that in each day evidence of the developmental, recreational, and corrective programs should be given. Obviously, some days you might devote all the time to one or two of the components. However, you should see evidence of each of the components when examining weekly or monthly teaching plans. The second area to consider relative to the question of time is the relative emphasis given to the two broad types of learnings, direct and inquiry, within the instructional program. Just as it is important to strike a balance between the three components of a subject or topic area, it is equally imperative that a balance be maintained within each subject area between direct and inquiry instruction. In addition, you should consider the time requirements for various skills within each of the two broad types of learning. Allocating sufficient time will depend on a host of factors, especially the complexity of the task, the context of instruction, and the characteristics of the students. Therefore, it is important to monitor instruction to ensure that you have allocated sufficient time for your students to learn.

Instructional Goals

One characteristic of effective teachers at every grade level is having a correct relationship to the two broad areas of learning (direct and inquiry), and this correct relationship is reflected in allocating sufficient time for both types of learning and using that time properly. Essentially, the different learnings require different teaching strategies, and these are ultimately reflected in the way time is used. Time for direct learnings is controlled and monitored very closely by the teacher, and all teacher-student interactions are assessed with time-on-task as the primary factor. Time is important to the development of inquiry learnings as well, but how that time is used is quite different. Whereas a high degree of quickly paced teacher-student interaction is considered crucial in direct instruction, in inquiry learning the key element is allowing students ample time in a variety of activities to develop higher-level thinking abilities. Productive time is certainly of concern, but not in the traditional sense of quickly paced instruction with the transmission model of instruction being used most of the time. For the development of inquiry goals, teachers assume the role of facilitator, not director. The teacher should indirectly monitor student involvement but, most importantly, allow time for student thinking and discovery without rescuing students. This time should include greater student participation and

Pause and Reflect: Self-Monitoring Activity 7.1

Classroom Discussion Time Allocation

Meaningful classroom discussions are essential to help students be engaged, comprehend ideas, and develop background knowledge. Complete a time study below indicating the activity, whether it was a direct or inquiry objective, and the amount of minutes directed to teacher–student discussion. Complete this assignment for two days, tabulate your results, and ask yourself if sufficient time was directed to teacher–student discussion for your activities.

Daily Activity	*Direct*	or	*Inquiry*	*Number of Minutes Devoted to Teacher–Student Discussion*
1. _____	_____		_____	_____
2. _____	_____		_____	_____
3. _____	_____		_____	_____
4. _____	_____		_____	_____
5. _____	_____		_____	_____
6. _____	_____		_____	_____
7. _____	_____		_____	_____
8. _____	_____		_____	_____
9. _____	_____		_____	_____
10. _____	_____		_____	_____

involvement in the application of ideas. Much more time needs to be allotted for independent activities in inquiry learnings than in direct learnings. There is also a distinction between goals of instruction and subsequent means of accomplishment in the two types of learning. In direct learning, application of a skill may take the form of a written assignment to be completed individually or in a cooperative group. In these cases there is a one-to-one correspondence between the goals of the lesson and the ensuing vehicle to practice the skill. In fostering inquiry learnings, it is most likely that a one-to-one correspondence between the goal and the activity will not be achieved. For example, if you want students to learn a problem-solving strategy, it is likely that students will work on various projects to demonstrate mastery rather than completing a worksheet. How much time is allocated to meet instructional goals and how that time is used are decisions over which teachers have control. Effective teachers assist students in becoming critical and creative learners. This means time is allocated and the use of that time is geared for developing thinking skills. In discussing this very point, Wassermann (1987) further stresses the importance of following through on a commitment to cultivate thinking in teaching.

> We must ask ourselves some hard questions. Do we really want students to think? Do we want them to become more critical and more questioning and less likely to accept things at face value? Do we want more critical debate in the classroom and less reliance on the teacher as the authority? In our hearts we may believe that we are in favor of thinking, but in our practice we tend to reward those students who sit quietly and don't ask the kinds of questions that make us uncomfortable, who give us the answers we want and accept what we say as truth, who do as they are told. To keep the classroom running smoothly, we demand conformity and avoid controversy. We choose solutions, not healthy skepticism. Unfortunately, we cannot have it both ways. We cannot have a thinking classroom without the mess that is an adjunct of any productive and creative art (p. 465).

Teachers who are convinced that inquiry learnings are worthwhile plan for students to be involved in various activities. Criteria that may be used to foster inquiry learnings are offered by Raths (1971). These criteria provide suggestions for modifying classroom activities to teach important learnings not given to specific behavioral objectives. As you design lessons on inquiry abilities, you are invited to employ one or more of these suggestions to make the learning more effective.

Criteria for Worthwhile Activities*

1. All other things being equal, one activity is more worthwhile than another if it permits children to make informed choices in carrying out the activity and to reflect on the consequences of their choices.

*From "Teaching without Specific Objectives" by J. Raths, 1971, *Educational Leadership,* 28, pp. 714–720. Copyright 1971 by the Association for Supervision and Curriculum Development. Reprinted by permission.

2. All other things being equal, one activity is more worthwhile than another if it assigns to students active roles in the learning situation rather than passive ones.

3. All other things being equal, one activity is more worthwhile than another if it asks students to engage in inquiry into ideas, applications of intellectual processes, or current problems, either personal or social.

4. All other things being equal, one activity is more worthwhile than another if it involves children with realia.

5. All other things being equal, one activity is more worthwhile than another if completion of the activity may be accomplished successfully by children at several different levels of ability.

6. All other things being equal, one activity is more worthwhile than another if it asks students to examine in a new setting and idea, an application of an intellectual process, or a current problem which has been previously studied.

7. All other things being equal, one activity is more worthwhile than another if it requires students to examine topics or issues that citizens in our society do not normally examine—and that are typically ignored by the major communication media in the nation.

8. All other things being equal, one activity is more worthwhile than another if it involves students and faculty members in "risk" taking—not a risk of life or limb, but a risk of success or failure.

9. All other things being equal, one activity is more worthwhile than another if it requires students to rewrite, rehearse, and polish their initial efforts.

10. All other things being equal, one activity is more worthwhile than another if it involves students in the application and mastery of meaningful rules, standards, or disciplines.

11. All other things being equal, one activity is more worthwhile than another if it gives students a chance to share the planning, the carrying out of a plan, or the results of an activity with others.

12. All other things being equal, one activity is more worthwhile than another if it is relevant to the expressed purposes of the students.

Collaborative Learning

As discussed in Chapter 6, cooperative learning opportunities are most effective in promoting both cognitive and social abilities of all students. Also, this grouping arrangement is particularly effective with culturally and linguistically diverse students. Cooperative grouping fosters greater peer interaction and learning and creates a team feeling among students. Although cooperative grouping takes different forms, one common procedure is to first give all students an explicit explanation of a skill or strategy and then form cooperative groups of students of varying abilities to work together on supervised and independent activities. Students are encouraged to help one another; they then receive a group evaluation or grade upon completion of the activity. Crucial to the success of cooperative grouping is the teacher's step-by-step modeling and guidance to students in how to conduct interpersonal relations and small-group interactions; the teacher must also monitor each group's effectiveness. The objective in cooperative grouping is to communicate to the students that they can achieve their goal by working with the other students within their group. In addition to cooperative grouping, other classroom arrangements to promote student engagement include small-group discussions. You are encouraged to try out cooperative grouping in your classroom and reflect on its implementation by responding to Pause and Reflect: Self-Monitoring Activity 7.2 (p. 117). Important findings from a recent study by Alvermann et al from the National Reading Research Center (1996) involving students of varying cultures and ethnicities highlighted the importance of small-group discussions over whole class discussions. As the authors stated in the R&D Watch (1996), "Small group discussions allow students more opportunities to talk and help students feel comfortable with each other, allowing them to take risks and share their thoughts" (p. 5).

Classroom Discussion

As with small-group instruction, teachers need to devote ample time to classroom discussions with students about what was read. The importance of interesting and meaningful discussions was covered in detail in Chapter 6. A further reminder of the importance of allocating classroom time to genuine dialogues between teachers and students comes from the previously mentioned study by Alvermann et al of the National Reading Research Center, which involved interviewing students of varying cultures and ethnicities. In summarizing the study, The R&D Watch (1996) reported:

> Students indicate that good discussions take place when everyone contributes, that is when all students have read the assignment and come prepared to discuss it. They must be responsible for listening to and questioning each other and keeping a focus on the topic. Students also note the fine line between respectfully discussing ideas that conflict and arguing (p. 5).

Differential Emphasis: Control of Instructional Activities and Learning Outcomes

As you spend time in various classrooms, you will inevitably observe a teacher in total control of the instructional activity at one time, imposing less control at other times, and engaging in little direct control of the learning task at still other times. Control in this sense means deciding what is being taught and how it is presented, practiced, and evaluated (as opposed to control of behavior and freedom of movement in the class). You might ask if this apparently fickle classroom behavior is desirable or if it is indicative of poor planning, resulting in wasted time. Such a pattern of teacher behavior is desirable and should become part of your repertoire. The underlying reason for this recommendation is that different degrees of teacher control of learning activities are necessary for achieving different instructional goals (Soar & Soar, 1983). Using one style of control for all types of instruction is not conducive to all types of learning. Studies on teacher effectiveness have indicated that just as you need to allocate sufficient time for students to learn different instructional goals, you also need to develop a sensitivity to varying control of the learning activity in relation to the cognitive level of the task at hand. Soar and Soar summarized this relationship well:

> For simple, low-cognitive-level outcomes, greater teacher control was best; but for more complex learning, less control was best. If the lesson was a rote one of memorizing the multiplication table or a list of spelling words, a closely structured drill would be appropriate. However, if pupils were solving complex problems or engaged in creative production, a much lower degree of control would be appropriate (p. 73).

The researchers point out that a teacher can go overboard and be too controlling in terms of the learning activity. Based on their investigations, they recommend a middle-of-the-road philosophy; that is, an intermediate amount of teacher control for greatest achievement gain. As we saw in Chapter 4, more control is generally needed for direct learnings and less control for developing inquiry learnings. This ability to shift one's control of the learning activity depending upon the type of instructional outcome will not be developed overnight, of course. As with the important yet painstaking skill of finding the correct pace for each lesson, it is safe to predict that acquiring this skill will take practice, trial and error, and more practice. If you are aware of this aspect of time management and monitor your growth in this area, however, you will continue to refine this skill. To reflect on your own teaching emphases, complete Pause and Reflect: Self-Monitoring Activity 7.3 (p. 119).

Pause and Reflect: Self-Monitoring Activity 7.2

Cooperative Learning Strategy

At the end of a teaching day, select a class in which you grouped students cooperatively to accomplish a learning goal. Respond to the following questions to reflect upon the effectiveness of the activity.

1. What criteria did you use in deciding the size and make-up of the cooperative groups?

2. What was the group goal and the criteria for success as a group?

3. As you monitored the groups working together, were all students actively engaged in learning?

4. How could you improve this activity the next time?

Pause and Reflect: Self-Monitoring Activity 7.3

Introspective View of Your Teaching

1. Review a lesson you recently taught. Does having students not actively engaged or off-task always indicate the same thing?   yes   no

   If your response is no, what are the different possibilities?

2. In your grade level and in a subject of your choice, do you feel there is sufficient balance between time allocated to developmental learning (including both direct and inquiry learnings) and to recreational learning independent activities (e.g., time for free reading, panel discussions, research projects, educational games)?   yes   no

   Why do you feel this way?

   Do you feel differently for other subjects?

3. Looking back over a full week of teaching, how did you find time to work with those students who are struggling to succeed?

   In retrospect, did you spend too little or too much time with these students?

   How can you solve this dilemma of providing individual help to your struggling students?

Self-Monitoring FYI: Time-on-Task

Definition: The amount of allocated time a student is actively working on the task at hand.

Tips:

- Be involved. That is the key to time-on-task. Students have to be involved with the teacher or the material, preferably the former. The more the teacher directs and guides, the better.
- Be sensitive to the pace of your lesson. Maintain a rapid pace but slow down or speed up when necessary.
- Provide academic-focused feedback during the teaching, supervised practice, and independent practice steps of direct instruction—the sooner, the better.
- Monitor independent seatwork. Be available to help students.
- Check to make sure students experience a high level of success with independent seatwork.
- Be certain your explanation of the skill and what you expect your students to accomplish are clear.
- Communicate to students what they are to do if they have a question while completing an independent assignment and what they are to do if they finish before the period is over.
- Be mindful of classroom management techniques from Chapter 5 (physical proximity, task-related comments, etc.).

Thinking Like a Teacher: Recap of Major Ideas

- Teachers have direct control over the quality of instructional time spent with students.
- Allocated time refers to the amount of time given to a particular subject.
- Academic engaged time, or time-on-task, refers to that portion of allocated time in which students work at the task at hand.
- It is recommended that you monitor how much time is allocated to: 1) various components in your subject area (developmental, independent, and corrective); 2) the two major types of learning (direct and inquiry); 3) peer and collaborative learning opportunities; and 4) genuine dialogue between you and your students with respect to class materials and readings.

Chapter EIGHT

Variety of Materials

When you begin the process of developing curriculum to use in the classroom, you will need to consider a classroom in which students of diverse backgrounds are not made to feel isolated or detached from the content. To meet the needs of students within a pluralistic classroom, effective teachers select and use a variety of instructional materials. As a part of these choices, teachers select appropriate materials that are consistent with culturally responsive instruction to capitalize on their efforts toward reflective decision making. These materials are then able to become vehicles in achieving instructional goals. Whether you are explaining a new skill, providing supervised or independent practice for a concept taught, creating higher-order tasks and authentic performances for small-group problem-solving, or fostering recreational reading opportunities, you and your students will be interacting with materials. Strategically applying a variety of materials that are culturally relevant in your classroom curriculum is a procedure you should do regardless of whether you teach high school science, middle school reading, or elementary school mathematics. This also applies to whether you teach in schools with predominantly one social group of students or many distinct social groups.

In addition to the materials chosen, your curriculum is not just the specific content you teach but the entire learning environment that is created by the visual and auditory materials used. Making arrangements for your instruction (yearly, by semester, monthly, weekly, and daily) will require you to plan with many types of materials in mind. Some examples of these varieties of materials include:

- Textbooks
- Supplemental texts and enrichment guides
- Reference books from differing sources
- Tradebooks and quality literature with diverse topics and authors
- Newspapers, magazines, and multiple types of periodicals
- Commercial learning kits and authentic reinforcement activities
- Realia: concrete objects, art work, math manipulatives, maps, charts, hands-on science experiments, diagrams, computers, tape recorders, calculators, television, cassettes/headphones, compact discs, videos, and microscopes; in addition, for kindergarten and primary grades (i.e., 1–3), cut-out letters, pictures, picture dictionaries, language-experience materials, games, bulletin board displays, and educational toys
- Teacher-made materials and ongoing assessments

Culturally Relevant Materials

When you attempt to use culturally relevant materials, you must consider the merits of connecting students' many cultures with all that goes on in your classroom on a daily basis. It is not sufficient for textbooks and other teaching materials to merely include content about various diverse groups; instead, the content about different populations should be an integral part and not an add-on or appendage. In many culturally insensitive settings it is common for content about people of color and/or women to be added to a textbook in a special section, as a special feature, or with inclusive photographs only. Teaching materials that view diversity in this way cannot be helpful in assisting students to reflect or rethink their experiences, to challenge their current assumptions, or to develop new perspectives and insights about differences and similarities.

In many school settings, the textbook is a prominent and primary tool for instruction and the exchange of content information. This means that the teacher must be able to consider the cultural sensitivity of textbooks used so that diverse groups of students can be meaningfully engaged. In many districts, however, this may be hindered when texts are chosen for particular schools, grade levels, and content areas without consultation or consideration of the teachers' needs or the needs of students that will be taught. This means that you may be limited in the types and variety of materials that you would like to use for students. When districts mandate the use of materials that are culturally distorted and potentially harmful for all students, teachers may feel resentful and devalued. A better way to address this dilemma is to know how to transform and supplement materials so that students can view concepts, issues, events, and themes from multiple perspectives.

How you actually use the curriculum materials or supplementary materials when interacting with students is another consideration. Most teachers recognize the potential benefits of using culturally relevant materials. For example, students tend to respond more positively when they can identify with the characters and events in the stories or expository information (Purves & Beach, 1972); students of diverse backgrounds can experience pride in their own identity and heritage when materials are factual or authentic (Harris, 1992); all students have opportunities to observe published authors from within multiple cultural groups and can be inspired to do their own writings; and differing students can be affirmed or validated in their personal experiences or divergent perspectives (Au, 1993). In addition, the appropriate use of culturally relevant materials presents all students with strategies to learn about the complexities of society as they develop respect and appreciation for those of other cultural groups (Walker-Dalhouse, 1992).

As you become interested in using culturally relevant materials, you will want to become familiar with some of the texts that are suitable for use at each grade level. Harris (1992) cautions that there are certain popular and critically acclaimed works that appear to deal with issues of diversity but do not meet the criteria for culturally sensitive literature. When you review materials, consider the challenging issues they raise and how you will handle these issues in discussions with your students.

Approaches for Teaching with Multicultural and Multiethnic Literature

There are four approaches that may be used with multicultural and multiethnic literature based on a hierarchy for integrating ethnic and cultural content in the curriculum (Banks, 1994; Rasinski & Padak, 1990). These are the *contributions*, *additive*, *transformative*, and *social action* approaches. These practices are different from traditional curriculum methods and use of materials because of their focus on issues of diversity and social justice within a democratic society.

The contributions approach familiarizes students with some multicultural content but does not necessarily lead them to examine their existing beliefs. It focuses on the process of interaction with materials centered around heroes, holidays, special customs, dress, foods, music, and other parts of a particular culture. Lessons using this approach will typically be directed toward topics such as Cinco de Mayo, Thanksgiving with the "Indians," Black History Month, or Chinese New Year. In this approach, students may read a biography of George Washington Carver, Caesar Chavez, or Chief Seattle. It is a convenient approach and materials may be plentiful, but the approach only gives students a superficial understanding of their own culture and the cultures of others. There is also a tendency to reinforce bias, stereotypes, and inappropriate beliefs, which can hinder a student's ability to respect and appreciate differences. The challenge for teachers with this approach is to develop deeper understandings of values and historical situations.

In the additive approach, concepts and content about other groups are added to the core curriculum instead of being treated separately. For instance, teachers may teach a lesson on folktales using diverse cultural literature such as *Mufaro's Beautiful Daughters* (Steptoe, 1987) or *Yeh Shen* (Louis, 1982) as examples of other versions of the Cinderella tale. The additive approach has benefits and limitations similar to those of the contributions approach. However, the basic structure of the curriculum remains unchanged using culturally diverse materials with the additive approach. Cultures are still viewed only from the mainstream perspective and without a focus on understanding the complex interrelationships between all groups.

The goals of the curriculum in the transformation approach are changed to study concepts, events, and issues from diverse perspectives, particularly those that tend to be omitted or misrepresented. For example, in a poetry unit you would select poetry written by members of a variety of groups. This method of teaching enables your students to explore various poetic forms as well as study those elements that are common to diverse poems. It is further recommended that the contributions and perspectives that you choose should depict each group as that particular group would depict itself. In this way, the representation is authentic, active, and dynamic. To make such selections, however, you must learn about various groups and become sensitive to aspects of each group's culture that are important to that group.

The following is another example of the use of the transformative approach: You may wish to include Native Americans in the curriculum materials and elect to study Sacajawea as a heroine to discuss. From the Native American perspective, however, Sequoya would be a preferable historic figure. Sacajawea served European American interests by leading Lewis and Clark west, whereas Sequoya served the interests of the Cherokee by developing an alphabet for encoding the Cherokee language.

Finally, the social action approach provides experiences for students to identify important social issues, gather information, clarify their values and assumptions, arrive at decisions, and take action to address the issues. The use of culturally relevant literature assists students in understanding and recognizing these social issues. For example, children in the primary grades may be introduced to the issues in the Civil Rights movement through *Rosa Parks,* a biography by Eloise Greenfield (1973). Students may discuss their own attitudes toward those of other ethnic or cultural groups, what it means to give equal rights to those of all groups, instances of discrimination in their own school or community, and the changes needed to correct these types of problems (Au, 1993). In addition, younger students can learn to debate and lobby for issues that are important to them. For example, the development of a proposal to get home and school rules changed to meet their interests and needs allows youngsters to become empowered in projects that directly affect them. Older students can engage in more sophisticated social action projects such as conducting a survey to determine the kinds of jobs that most ethnic minority groups have in local hotels, restaurants, and firms; and, if necessary, urging local businesses to hire more ethnic minorities in top-level positions. These students could also choose to make recommendations regarding changes to be made in the laws or the ways in which laws should be implemented, with the final outcome being a presentation of these recommendations to appropriate public officials (Banks, 1981).

A number of curriculum guides are available to teachers to help them teach students social action skills. For example, the Martin Luther King, Jr. Center on Nonviolent Social Change has developed a curriculum guide to infuse Dr. King's principles of nonviolent social action into the curriculum (Sleeter & Grant, 1993). The teaching guide *Open Minds to Equality* (Schniedewind & Davidson, 1983) provides a step-by-step series of activities to build group cooperation, then collective skills in analysis of local issues and taking action. *The Kid's Guide to Social Action* (Lewis, 1991) shows young people how to take various kinds of actions such as writing letters, organizing petitions, and making persuasive speeches. A number of other materials are available that serve as guidelines for educators to ensure that textbooks and other instructional materials reflect the racial and ethnic diversity of our society and its past. Some considerations may include: *Ten Quick Ways to Analyze Children's Books* (Council on Interracial Books for Children, reprint); "Evaluate your Textbooks for Racism and Sexism," in Maxine Dunfee's (Ed.), *Eliminating Ethnic Bias in Instructional Materials: Comment and Bibliography* (Rosenberg, 1974).

A strength of the social action approach is that it allows students to sharpen their thinking, develop research skills, search for solutions to real-life problems, and understand that they can make a difference. At its highest level, this approach requires much effort for teachers to plan wisely and organize units or thematic instruction. A greater issue for you is the possibility of controversial topics; it is important to be aware of how to handle the sensitivities of students, parents, and other educators. Teachers who utilize the social action approach are communicating commitment and enabling students to explore in thoughtful and positive ways for the equitable treatment and well-being of all groups. The use of materials, in this last approach, has the effect of assisting students in reflecting on beliefs, values, and practices that affect their own lives as well as the lives of others.

Pause and Reflect Self-Monitoring Activity 8.1 (p. 129) provides you an opportunity to reflect on the prior school experiences you had with multicultural and multiethnic literature.

Computer-Assisted Instruction (CAI)

The emergence of computers in our schools and classrooms has led to one indisputable fact: opportunities for students to interact with a computer for instructional purposes are now available and increasingly broadened with the incorporation of internet and on-line programming. Computers are utilized for several purposes in our schools, including assessment and reporting, computerized strategies for instruction, and management of ongoing instructional decision-making using anecdotal records.

As teachers-in-preparation, you may have several primary concerns:

1. In what ways can the computer be integrated into the instructional program to enhance student learning?

2. How effective is computer-assisted instruction [CAI] in terms of student reaction and achievement in a particular subject area?

3. How effective is the software, and who decides which programs students will complete?

The first concern is addressed by examining your instructional goals and deciding how computers can assist in their development. You will need to try out ways of incorporating computers into your class and monitoring their effectiveness. The second concern can be assessed through both informal and formal assessment. The third concern deals directly with the quality of computer software. In this regard, computers should be treated like any other instructional materials, and they should be viewed as vehicles to assist you in accomplishing your instructional goals. Whether or not CAI will be a positive experience for students will mainly depend on the quality of the software and how that software is utilized. There are numerous software programs in every subject, and more are being developed in mass production.

There are four types of software programs: drill-and-practice, tutorial, simulation, and games. The majority of software programs for the classroom are in the form of drill and skill (e.g., electronic ditto sheet). These programs are designed to practice and reinforce skills previously introduced by teachers but not mastered by students. In a typical sequence in this form of computer-assisted instruction, a question is presented on the screen, the student responds, and the computer answers "correct," "incorrect," or "let's try again." Many drill-and-practice programs provide teachers with a report card detailing the percentage of items answered correctly and significant error patterns.

Tutorial software programs not only provide practice but carry on a dialogue with students by giving an explanation of a skill. The tutorial program is more complex than the drill-and-practice program, since there is more interaction between the computer and the student. When an incorrect response is made by the student, the tutorial program will indicate that the response is incorrect, explain why it is incorrect, reteach the skill, and give the student a similar item to attempt. Simulation software presents hypothetical situations that require students to respond. These programs have more inherent motivational value than either of the previously mentioned types and offer a unique method to develop thinking skills and problem-solving abilities. Learning games are a popular type of software program that usually employs a drill-and-practice format to practice previously introduced skills.

Quantity of software is not a major problem for most teachers, but quality is. You must exercise your knowledge of the subject area and of the students to select appropriate software. One overriding recommendation is to always try the software yourself before buying it and requiring students to spend instructional time with it. Figure 8.1 (p. 131) presents a software selection guide, examining the type of program, ease of use, instructional design, content accuracy, and special features. Computers are in the schools! However, you need to exercise control over how they are used in your subject area and which programs will be used with students.

Quantity versus Quality Dilemma

Effective teachers use a greater variety of materials in their content areas to engage their students in learning than less effective teachers do. In reality, the use of a variety of materials is intertwined with each principle of instruction—affective engagement, classroom management and organization, culturally responsive instruction, quality time, multiple assessments, and teacher expectations. A teacher may have the best intentions, but if the appropriate materials are not used in the proper fashion, positive results will not follow.

Instructional materials are a potent part of the learning process. In fact, the abundance of diverse materials for every content area on the market today is astounding. The teacher can very easily become overwhelmed with their completeness and attach an unwarranted and naive emphasis to them. Quantity of instructional materials is not an issue but, unfortunately, such is not the case with quality. You must be wary of using fancy-looking materials without first determining their quality. You have a great deal of control over this aspect of teaching. Moreover, you should first make sure you understand the purpose of any intended instructional material. At times, materials are unduly criticized because they were not successful for a particular situation when, in fact, that was not the intended purpose of the materials. Second, make sure the materials are accurate. Do not assume accuracy—you are the expert. Many times, instructional materials contain inaccurate information or make faulty assumptions regarding prerequisite

Pause and Reflect: Self-Monitoring Activity 8.1

Journal Entry: Thinking Back on Prior Experiences

- Reflect back to the materials and books that you used when you were in elementary, middle, and high school. Did you read and discuss any multicultural and multiethnic literature in class? If so, how did you and your classmates respond? Would your responses be different now?

- If you did not read any multicultural and multiethnic literature, why do you think this was so? What are the possible effects of the lack of use of a variety of materials from diverse perspectives on you and your classmates?

- What implications can you draw from these responses for your own teaching today?

Type of Program	Good	Adequate	Poor
_____ Drill and Practice	_____	_____	_____
_____ Tutorial	_____	_____	_____
_____ Simulation	_____	_____	_____
_____ Learning Game	_____	_____	_____
Ease of Use/User Friendly			
Clear Directions	_____	_____	_____
Exit Capabilities	_____	_____	_____
Control of Pacing	_____	_____	_____
Provision of Help	_____	_____	_____
Instructional Design			
Objective Clearly Stated	_____	_____	_____
Introductory Explanation	_____	_____	_____
Sample Exercises	_____	_____	_____
Number of Practice Exercises	_____	_____	_____
Immediate/Varied Feedback	_____	_____	_____
Branching Capability	_____	_____	_____
Built-In Assessment of Progress	_____	_____	_____
Monitoring of Student Responses	_____	_____	_____
Corrections Made by Reteaching, Giving Clues, or Explaining Skill	_____	_____	_____
Summary Statement	_____	_____	_____
Length of Program	_____	_____	_____
Appropriate Difficulty Level	_____	_____	_____
Authentic Content			
Direct Correspondence between Lesson Object, Lesson Procedures, and Real-Life Skill	_____	_____	_____
Accuracy	_____	_____	_____
Procedures Reflect What a Reader Has to Do in the Processes of Reading	_____	_____	_____
Before, during, and after Reading Activities	_____	_____	_____
Effective Sequencing	_____	_____	_____
Special Features			
Graphics	_____	_____	_____
Animation	_____	_____	_____
Speech	_____	_____	_____
Music	_____	_____	_____
Compact Discs	_____	_____	_____
Touch Screen	_____	_____	_____
Laser Videodiscs	_____	_____	_____
Audio	_____	_____	_____
Color	_____	_____	_____

FIGURE 8.1 Software Selection Guide

Heilman/Blair/Rupley, PRINCIPLES AND PRACTICES OF TEACHING READING, 8/e 1993, p. 296.
Reprinted by permission of Prentice Hall, Upper Saddle River, New Jersey.

knowledge that students should possess to be successful with the new content. You must develop a self-monitoring, reflecting, and discriminating attitude toward instructional materials to ensure the quality of your instruction. Though materials are important in achieving instructional goals, you must always remember that materials are effective only in the hands of a capable teacher. Materials themselves are ineffective and can actually hinder student learning. However, the effective teacher uses materials in just the right way to "unbank the fire" and to achieve learning goals. In this sense, effective teachers always maintain a correct relationship to materials; that is, they utilize materials as their aids in realizing instructional goals. It is easy to become an assistant to materials, and guarding against this pitfall is becoming more important today. Pressures are acute to follow a standard type of instruction by blindly utilizing materials to ensure student mastery of basic skills. This is not effective or culturally responsive teaching. In this scenario the teacher is merely a technician. The effective teacher, however, selects and modifies materials to meet the needs of students. Adjusting educational materials to do this is sound educational practice.

Personalizing Your Teaching

Effective teachers produce their own materials to help meet the specific needs of diverse groups of students. It is unrealistic to assume that all students will profit equally from using the same textbooks or other types of materials. The necessity for modifying and adapting existing materials and creating new materials comes as a result of:

1. Range/demands of your instructional purposes (culturally relevant, developmental, recreational, corrective)
2. Student variability (instructional level, preferred learning styles, interests)
3. Unique aspects of the community and current events (city, state, national, global)

Designing and devising your own materials will meet these three major requirements. As a consequence, instructional time tends to be used wisely because students will likely be motivated to learn and interested in learning because you are personalizing instruction. As you know, teachers try their best to implement their assessment information and use appropriate materials and activities to meet student needs. You must be certain that the materials are accomplishing instructional goals. The better the match between materials and instructional goals, the better the chances for improved student learning. Your judgments are crucial in this area. Being creative and designing materials specific to your curriculum will allow students to be more successful.

The best uses of materials often come about when teachers modify the original purpose of commercial materials to create a more meaningful and creative application. Students can become actively involved in learning if materials are manipulated to fit their needs. This is precisely why teacher-made materials are so effective. It is also a good idea to ask students how to modify instructional materials and to remember that the teacher's manual for a given set of materials does not know your students, your philosophical stance, or your program. Keep notes on ways in which experienced teachers in your school have modified instructional materials.

It is also important to motivate students before using any type of materials. Very few materials are, by themselves, engaging or motivating. Time spent in preparing and motivating students to work with materials will pay off in student involvement and learning. The best materials are only as good as the teacher who is using them. In the hands of an exciting teacher, even dull materials can come alive and be effective in the classroom.

The ways to modify existing materials and types of teacher-made materials are limited only by your imagination. The following are some examples:

Comprehension activities

Functional activities

Vocabulary games

Word identification games

Language arts materials

Math manipulatives

Language experience books

Learning centers

Action research projects

Art/music/drama enrichments

Modification of existing textbooks

- Advanced organizers
- Graphic/visual organizers
- Reader guides
- Structured overviews
- Audiotaping of informational texts
- Changing the stated directions to fit students' needs and instructional goals

The key to producing effective teacher-made materials is to realize that you know your students and program better than any set of materials does. Work toward using a blend of commercial and teacher-made materials in the classroom. The following self monitoring FYI gives you a list of possible concerns to consider in the selection of materials to be used in your classroom.

Self-Monitoring FYI: Selecting and Evaluating Materials

Key concerns for selection of materials to be used in a diverse classroom:
- Do the materials reflect student interests and preferred mode of learning or both?
- Do the materials represent a variety of readability levels to match student abilities?

- Do the materials relate directly to your instructional goals, themes, and outcomes or do the materials reinforce and extend what students need to know?
- Are the materials applicable to flexible groupings that you anticipate using (cooperative, large, individual, small)?
- Do the materials follow an acceptable sequence for culturally responsive practices?
- Do you need to supply feedback, or are the materials self-correcting in nature?
- Is sufficient information presented to develop your content to acceptable levels of proficiency for all students?
- Can all students feel pride in their own identity and heritage from the materials chosen?
- Do the materials offer a complete and balanced view of the historical forces that shaped society in this country?
- Can materials be used to explore issues of social justice?

Pause and Reflect Self-Monitoring Activity 8.2 is a classroom materials inventory to assist you in the evaluation of materials you are using in your classroom.

Thinking Like a Teacher: Recap of Major Ideas

- To meet the needs of students within a pluralistic classroom, effective teachers select and use a variety of instructional materials.
- The use of a variety of materials is intertwined with each principle of instruction—affective engagement, classroom management and organization, culturally responsive instruction, quality time, multiple assessments, and teacher expectations.
- Your curriculum is not just the specific content you teach, but the entire learning environment that is created by the visual and auditory materials that are used.
- It is not sufficient for textbooks and other teaching materials to merely include content about various diverse groups; instead, the content about different populations should be an integral part.
- Although the textbook is a prominent and primary tool for instruction and the exchange of content information in most school settings, know how to transform and supplement materials so that students can view concepts, issues, events, and themes from multiple perspectives.
- There are four approaches that may be used with multicultural literature. These are the *contributions*, *additive*, *transformative*, and *social action* approaches.

Pause and Reflect: Self-Monitoring Activity 8.2

Journal Entry: Classroom Materials Inventory

Collect the materials that are used in the classroom in which you are working. For each material, decide if its purpose is developmental (the primary text(s) of the subject) practice (material used for application or reinforcement) recreational (material used for fostering independent skills, abilities, and attitudes) or culturally relevant (material that is authentic, real-life, and meaningful). After making this decision, write the name of the material under the appropriate heading. For each material, cite the assumption(s) underlying its philosophy or use with students and primary advantages. Indicate the limitations of each material in the last column.

Classroom Materials Inventory Form

Purpose	*Assumptions Underlying Usage*	*Advantages*	*Limitations*

Developmental Materials

_____	_____	_____	_____
_____	_____	_____	_____
_____	_____	_____	_____
_____	_____	_____	_____
_____	_____	_____	_____

Practice Materials

_____	_____	_____	_____
_____	_____	_____	_____

Continued

Purpose	Assumptions Underlying Usage	Advantages	Limitations
_____	_____	_____	_____
_____	_____	_____	_____
_____	_____	_____	_____

Recreational Materials

_____	_____	_____	_____
_____	_____	_____	_____
_____	_____	_____	_____
_____	_____	_____	_____

Culturally Relevant/Authentic Materials

_____	_____	_____	_____
_____	_____	_____	_____
_____	_____	_____	_____
_____	_____	_____	_____

- Use a variety of materials that allow students to sharpen their thinking; develop research skills; search for solutions to challenging, real-life problems; and understand that they can make a difference.
- Whether or not computer-assisted instruction will be a positive experience for students will mainly depend on the quality of the software and how that software is utilized.
- Always try the software yourself before buying it and requiring students to spend instructional time with it.
- Make sure you understand the purpose of any intended instructional material.
- The best materials are only as good as the teacher who is using them.
- The key to producing effective teacher-made materials is to realize that you know your students and program better than any set of materials does.

Chapter NINE

Assessment and Instructional Decision-Making

Assessment is one of the most important and pressing issues facing educators. If teachers at any grade level are going to help students become thoughtful, critical, responsive, and effective as learners, the decisions teachers make about instruction need to be made on diagnostic information. Research on teaching has reaffirmed the widely accepted belief in the importance of educational diagnosis (Fisher et al., 1980). As emphasized earlier, research on teaching has yielded no simple recipe for teaching success. However, it has revealed that because students, content areas, and instructional goals are different, effective teaching methods will vary. Inherent in this statement is the necessity for effective assessment as a prerequisite for good teaching.

Dozens of new assessment initiatives have been implemented in the past several years. Yet, for assessment to be effective and feasible, we need descriptions and perspectives; we need to know what the assessments look like, how they are constructed and used, and their intended purposes. Without reflection and an understanding of assumptions and processes, we will not be able to design assessments that accomplish the intended goals.

Educational assessment is a process that permeates all instruction. It can be defined as a process whereby students' strengths and challenges in a given area are determined. Effective teachers collect relevant information on students, interpret and synthesize this information, and instruct according to student needs. They continually evaluate and reshape teaching decisions depending on a student's progress. Thus, the assessment process intrinsically affects the entire teaching-learning cycle. Underlying this process is a deep respect for the individual student. By seeking and utilizing assessment information to plan culturally responsive instruction, teachers are communicating a compassionate and respectful attitude toward the teaching-learning situation. Figure 9.1 illustrates how assessment is an integral part of all facets of teaching.

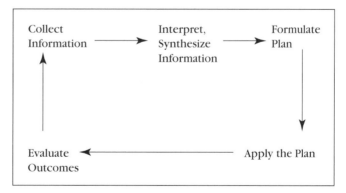

FIGURE 9.1   Cycle of Educational Assessment

Some of the decisions or actions that depend on diagnostic assessment processes are:

Deciding on the content of lesson plans

Determining the types of questions to ask students

Determining the type of homework to be assigned

Analyzing the essential components of an intended thematic unit

Developing the teacher-made materials for instructional purposes

Deciding on various informal and formal techniques

Deciding on the initial placement of a student in a class

Deciding when to reteach a particular skill or concept

Designing assessments at the end of a lesson or thematic unit

Reporting a student's progress

Determining the content of class handout sheets

Recommending students for special services (i.e., gifted and talented, remedial and intervention)

Increasing student motivation

Constructing teacher-made tests and assessments

Pinpointing areas causing difficulty in a content area

Determining the effectiveness of a particular teaching strategy

Determining how well instructional goals have been mastered

In relation to the two broad types of learnings discussed in Chapter 6—direct and inquiry—basing instruction on diagnostic information will help you to keep clearly in mind what you want students to learn. Being able to justify why you are doing what you are doing is one characteristic of an effective teacher. Guiding students in an inquiry ability, such as classifying information into meaningful categories, requires you to assess students' entry abilities carefully and plan activities that will challenge them to think as well as capitalize on the strengths of others while working in cooperative group settings. Research on teaching direct learnings has supported the importance of diagnosis on increasing student time-on-task. One of the components of a high percentage of academic learning time is that students enjoy a high success rate (or low error rate). The probability for success is raised for a given task if students work on a "just right" (instructional) level. Without initial and continual diagnosis of students' abilities, the likelihood of success and a high time-on-task percentage is not favorable. Working at one's frustration level (i.e., when the work is too difficult) all but eliminates the chance of producing significant achievement in direct learnings. Also, the crucial components of monitoring student progress and providing feedback in the direct instruction model are based on the teacher's ability to accurately diagnose and respond to student progress.

Being an effective diagnostician will enable you to match classroom instruction to instructional goals. Given the nature of individual as well as cultural, socioeconomic, and linguistic differences, it is important to realize that different levels of diagnosis as well as multiple types of assessments are required for students with diverse learning needs. Classroom teachers are expected to diagnose their class at an analytical level at the beginning of the school year and to diagnose students' progress continuously throughout the school year. An analytical level of diagnosis requires teachers to be able to make four types of decisions:

1. To determine the general achievement levels in the class
2. To identify individual differences within the class
3. To determine the needs of the class
4. To identify students in need of further diagnosis

Standardized and Criterion-Referenced Tests

These four decisions can be made based on a combination of formal and informal measures and teacher observations. Formal measures include standardized achievement tests and commercially prepared criterion-referenced tests. Because you have probably studied educational assessment in other coursework, it is not the intention of this section to delve into this area in detail. However, for purposes of review and reflection, a brief comparison between standardized achievement and criterion-referenced tests is presented.

Standardized achievement tests are used with the rationale that these tests interpret an individual's knowledge of content information on the basis of the performance of other students of the same age (norm group) on the same test. The purpose of these tests are to measure what students have learned in a specific subject. Performance is reported in a variety of forms including raw scores, percentiles, percentile bands, stanines, and grade equivalents (e.g., Comprehensive Test of Basic Skills [CTBS], Stanford Achievement Test, Iowa Test of Basic Skills, SRA Achievement Series, Sequential Test of Educational Progress [STEP]).

The rationale for criterion-referenced tests is to measure a student's performance with regard to an objective or criterion. The purpose of these tests are to assess which student objectives have been achieved in a specific subject. Performance is reported by the results of a percentage of questions answered correctly for each specific objective and the total number of objectives mastered (e.g., Objective-Referenced Bank of Items and Test [ORBIT] [CTB/McGraw-Hill], state-mandated basic skills tests, minimum competency tests, commercially prepared reading and math skill-assessment programs, teacher-prepared tests to determine if students have reached a desired standard or criterion in a specific area).

Most achievement tests provide "ballpark" information on students; that is, on their general achievement levels. Thus, these are survey tests indicating overall achievement levels. However, some standardized tests furnish information on students' performance by breaking down a subject area into component parts and providing separate subscores on each component in addition to an overall score. Such specific information on students is valuable in making diagnostic decisions for instruction.

Since new tests are continually being developed and old tests revised, it is difficult to remain current with all the standardized and criterion-referenced tests in many areas. Two excellent sources of information about tests are the professional journals in your area and *Mental Measurement Yearbook*, edited by Buros (1984). This volume, updated annually, is probably the most authoritative source of information on published tests. It contains test reviews by recognized authorities in the field of assessment and is available in the reference section of most libraries.

Rethinking Standardized Tests

Recently, however, numerous reports have documented the negative consequences of overreliance on traditional formal tests (Cannel, 1988; Darling-Hammond & Wise, 1985; Linn, Graue, & Sanders, 1990; Smith, 1991). First, there is a growing awareness that these types of tests do not capture the higher-level literacy abilities needed for participation in the workplace. Standardized tests do not adhere to our present research-based understanding of the complex processes of literacy and learning within the content areas. In addition, they are not aligned with daily classroom instructional procedures. Many times, teachers may look to the content or actual items of tests as a concrete indication of what they should teach (Koretz, 1991; Shepard, 1989). The results of such thinking has had a narrowing effect on curricula and fragmentation of teaching and learning (Linn, 1985).

Assessment that encompasses students' past, present, and future literacy development is an important concern for classroom teachers. This idea of time helps to clarify some of the problems associated with how we measure development with traditional forms of assessment. For example, the teacher observes students' reading development as they work through various classroom reading activities during day-to-day classroom instruction. The teacher may form a valid perception of what and how students are learning as they collaborate and performance is observed. However, when the end-of-the-year standardized achievement tests in reading are given, it may be found that the students' scores fall below their reading performance observed in the classroom. The standardized test measures the students' past reading development, whereas the teacher's analysis includes the total of their past, present, and emerging future development.

Many times teachers and students feel they are passive recipients and targets of assessment rather than active participants and partners in the process when tests are used as measures of accountability. Critical results of these assessments may be received when they are no longer timely or relevant to instructional decisions. Thus, results may not be meaningful for teachers seeking information on the effectiveness of their instruction or for students seeking feedback on their progress. Finally, dependency on standardized tests has led many policymakers and teachers to discount assessment because of inconsistencies based on a single indicator of accomplishment rather than multiple indicators.

Since there has been a rethinking of traditional formal assessment usage, attention has turned increasingly to other measures of assessment (e.g., portfolios or collections of student work, projects, and written responses encountered naturally in class). Policymakers, measurement specialists, and educators have taken seriously the need for better assessment and, as a result, we now find ourselves in the midst of a movement to develop what has become known as authentic assessment.

Authentic Assessment and Portfolios

Assessment that is authentic focuses on higher-level literacy abilities using "real life" literacy tasks and actual classroom artifacts and/or projects as part of the emphasis. These types of assessments use the active engagement of teachers and students in the assessment process while acknowledging the different needs of policymakers, the community, school personnel and students (e.g., interest/attitudinal surveys, observational checklists, formal and informal interviews, conference forms, think-aloud protocols, learning logs, detailed/focused observations, anecdotal record-keeping, analyses of records from projects, cooperative group activities, and writing folders). The list of authentic assessment activities is a long one. However, unless goals and outcomes are kept foremost in educators' minds, authentic assessment will probably not be different from standardized tests. If this happens, the techniques of assessment, rather than the rationale, will drive the system.

Authentic assessment allows teachers to assess many different dimensions of literacy and content area concepts, the potential to use classroombased information, the capacity to involve students in their own evaluation, and the use of multiple measures of students' abilities. However, authentic assessment should not be equated with a lack of standards. To the contrary, in authentic assessment the standards are those that truly matter in the workplace settings. All students can strive to attain high standards if the assessments are used to instruct rather than categorize.

Portfolios are collections of authentic tasks gathered across time and across contexts. The use of portfolios and other current trends in authentic assessment comes from a widespread dissatisfaction with more traditional methods of assessment, which include standardized achievement tests; criterion-referenced tests; unit tests in commercial reading series; science and social studies unit tests; diagnostic tests; and even teacher-designed, objective, multiple-choice tests (e.g., Haney & Madaus, 1989; Johnston, 1984; Miller-Jones, 1989; Nickerson, 1989; Resnick & Resnick, 1990; Shepard, 1989; Suhor, 1985). As an assessment instrument, it is a tool to expand the quantity and quality of information we use to examine student learning and growth.

As a type of authentic assessment, portfolio tasks are representative of the ways that people use reading and writing in the real world. For example, a literacy portfolio may contain lists of books read for pleasure, drafts of letters and manuscripts, final copies of exemplary pieces of work, the results of reading or writing conferences, and other kinds of evidence of literacy gathered over time. In the same respect, portfolios in math, science, or other content areas may each look very different. Thus, it is helpful to think of authentic assessment as a class of performance types and portfolios as one member of that class. It is also important to note that the use of portfolios does not necessarily preclude the use of other kinds of assessments, including other types of performance assessments (Winograd & Jones, 1992).

Types of Portfolios

One of the most popular types of portfolios is a *best pieces* portfolio, which contains examples of work that the student (sometimes with help from the teacher) considers to be his or her best efforts. Best pieces portfolios exhibit popularity because they encourage students to become more reflective about and involved in their own learning. Indeed, a number of writers argue that what makes a portfolio a portfolio is that these collections include "student participation in selecting contents, the criteria for selection, the criteria for judging merit, and evidence of student self-evaluation" (Paulson, Paulson, & Meyer, 1991, p. 60).

Another kind of portfolio that is in use around the country is a *descriptive portfolio,* which enables teachers to gather a wide variety of measures on the children they teach. These portfolios may include self-portraits drawn by the child; interviews with the child and with the parents; and the results of informal assessments such as Concepts About Print Test, a reading sample, and a writing sample. Many teachers are familiar with *process portfolios,* which are an intrinsic part of the writing process advocated by people like Graves (1983), Hansen (1987), and others. Process portfolios can contain a variety of products, including finished projects, manuscripts in progress, plans for topics of future papers, and lists identifying ways in which the student has grown as a reader and a writer.

Finally, a number of states are requiring teachers to gather *accountability portfolios.* These may be collections that include a table of contents; a best piece of work; a letter to the reviewer telling why the piece was selected as one of the best; a short story, poem, or play; a personal narrative; and other writing samples. This portfolio, along with writing samples done on demand, may then provide part of the basis to determine the quality of instruction. Best pieces portfolios, descriptive portfolios, process portfolios, or accountability portfolios are not the only kinds of portfolios in use, nor are they pure types that are clearly distinct from each other. More importantly, teachers and students often find that the portfolios they use in class may serve different functions at different times. In actual use, it is often hard to categorize portfolios as purely a best pieces, descriptive, or process (Winograd & Jones, 1992).

Cultural Bias in Assessment

A review of the literature on cultural bias in tests reveals that standardized achievement test scores often make a major difference in where children are placed in school programs. Critics of these tests charge that the tests are culturally biased against racial, ethnic, and economic minorities. That is, for racial minorities, ethnic groups, and low socioeconomic classes, the tests usually yield significantly lower results than for mainstream students. The overrepresentation of these groups in special education has been well documented.

Sociocultural factors that may cause bias in test results include language or dialect variations, test content, motivation, and attitudes toward the testing situation or context. When the test results are used for placements or to allot resources, the potential exists for discrimination against those of lower socioeconomic classes or minorities. The labeling of diverse groups of children as inferior, deficient, or slow should be considered a major problem for education. For example, Toni Morrison's novel *The Bluest Eye* (1970) poignantly shows the grievous wounds a society can inflict, saddling its victims with a crippling self-hatred. The protagonist of the book, Pecola, an African American adolescent, actually goes insane because she does not have the blue eyes of the "prettier, blond white girl" who is idolized by the media. Culturally different children have not fared well under the "melting pot" theory of education, which emphasizes deficits rather than recognizing and applauding differences. Although the goal of the assessment process should be to provide appropriate instruction, the cruel reality is that for many children, diagnosis is nothing more than a classification process for students who are diverse in language, race/ethnicity, socioeconomic status, or other ways.

Informal Assessments

Informal assessment measures include teacher-made tests, various checklists for particular behaviors, skill inventories, interest inventories, and daily assignments. Placing students in the proper level of instructional materials (i.e., at the instructional level) is an important step in ensuring successful learning. If students are trying to learn from materials that are too difficult for them (that is, at their frustration level), it is safe to predict that few will be as successful as they should be in learning. Matching the difficulty or readability level of class materials to your students' performance level should be one of your concerns throughout the year. One way to determine which students can be successful with a particular content textbook at the beginning of the year is to devise a teacher-made content-area reading inventory (Vacca & Vacca, 1986).

This approach is applicable for content subjects from grades four through twelve. The authors suggest the inventory be used at the beginning of either a course or an instructional unit and that the inventory focus on assessing students' skills at locating information, comprehension abilities, vocabulary skills, and reading rate. Locational skills are assessed by first determining the particular skills (e.g., the use of maps, diagrams, index, library materials) needed in the subject and then by preparing exercises that require students to show their competence in using contextual clues, their knowledge of word structure, and their dictionary skills.

Determining students' strengths and challenges in the area of comprehension can be accomplished by selecting a passage from the text of 500 to 1,000 words and composing ten to fifteen comprehension questions for the students to answer. Students are to read the passage silently and answer the questions. These questions should assess the types of skills you deem important in your subject area and should span the different levels of comprehension (literal, interpretative, and critical). By counting the total number of words in the passage and providing each student with his or her silent reading time using a stopwatch, you will be able to determine both a percentage of comprehension questions answered correctly and a reading rate. Students answering at least 75 percent of the questions correctly will most likely be successful in reading and learning from that particular content textbook. To ascertain the proper beginning or placement level for elementary students in reading and math, it is recommended that you administer one of a variety of informal reading inventories or criterion-referenced pretests (see Heilman, Blair, & Rupley, 1986).

Advantages of teacher-made diagnostic tests over standardized tests include the ability to note more specific strengths and challenges, to more readily establish groups from information collected, and to more closely measure small increments of growth. Teacher-made tests are by far the best measures of general and specific achievement levels in class, of determining appropriate learning activities, and of ascertaining if your instructional goals have been achieved.

Thus, not only at the beginning of the year but throughout the year, teacher-made tests are best for assessing if students have achieved your objectives, because your own tests will mirror instruction far better than any standardized test. Teacher-made tests will provide valuable diagnostic information that should improve not only your students' learning but your teaching as well. Because of the nature of teacher-made tests, the amount of information they will yield far outdistances standardized tests. Extreme care should be given in designing test items that accurately reflect your instruction. In addition, careful analysis of the test results vis-a-vis item difficulty and class response patterns can help in evaluating the results (Carlson, 1985).

Other forms of informal measures are daily assignment sheets and handouts for homework. Much diagnostic information can be gleaned from these sources besides total percentage of correct responses. As with teacher-made tests, item difficulty and individual and group response patterns can provide you with diagnostic information both to modify instruction and to improve future assignments.

This Pause and Reflect Self-Monitoring Activity 9.1 provides you an opportunity to interpret information and plan instruction based on assessment data.

Teacher Observation

The most powerful diagnostic tool is keen teacher observation. If you really observe, know what to look for, what to listen for and then translate this information into instructional decisions, you will be able to better match your

Pause and Reflect: Self-Monitoring Activity 9.1

Diagnostic Assessment

Gather standardized and informal test data on a randomly chosen student in the classroom (remember to maintain the anonymity of the student). Use test data and other significant information to prescribe an instructional program for the student.

Diagnostic Data

1. Test data (list test and scores or results)

2. Insights from your observation of students

3. Student interests (utilize interests inventories)

4. Student strengths

5. Student challenges

6. Preferred cognitive learning style

Continued

Instructional Decision-Making

1. Instructional goal

2. Level of material appropriate for instruction

3. Special materials and activities

4. Motivational strategies

5. Type of adjustment to ensure success

teaching techniques to student needs. In this sense, observation becomes a teaching tool. In reality, it must be acknowledged that some teachers can spend all day with students but not really see or know them. To really observe you must be armed with the knowledge of essential learnings in your content area, possess a basic understanding of the culturally developmental characteristics of students, and focus your attention on a specific area.

Observation in three areas—of students, of the classroom, and of one's own teaching—can yield valuable diagnostic information. Observing students during instruction can help pinpoint their strengths and challenges. A teacher may informally observe and note student responses or use a structured observation scale. The overriding criterion is knowing precisely what you are observing.

Understanding the effect of the classroom environment on student learning is important to providing good instruction. The seating arrangements, use of classroom space, different grouping plans, and sound levels can be observed informally or in a more structured fashion. Many times a change in the physical environment will affect student learning, either positively or negatively.

Looking at one's own teaching is sometimes called diagnosis of instruction. Too often we only look at students and never examine ourselves and our programs. Pause and Reflect: Self-Monitoring Activities are aimed at diagnosis of instruction and at encouraging you to develop this habit of looking at yourself as well as at your students.

Observation is a powerful tool for classroom teachers when information from each of the three areas is combined with personal and background knowledge of strengths and challenges. However, since you will be grouping students for various purposes, it is also important to be able to survey the performance of an entire class and to determine achievement levels and common patterns of need. For this reason, it is helpful to design a class record sheet with specific information from various sources on each student. By profiling the abilities of the entire class, it facilitates making the four analytical diagnostic decisions.

The ability to translate these observations into meaningful classroom experiences would be weakened if you did not "know" your students. This "knowing" involves gathering background information (test scores, anecdotal records, portfolios, special learning characteristics) and learning personal characteristics (home background, family members, interests, attitudes, motivation). Your ability to relate to your students, to motivate them to learn, and to select appropriate learning experiences will be based on this diagnostic process. As previously stressed, it is one matter to collect necessary information on students and the learning situation but quite another to use the information collected appropriately. The quality of classroom time is dependent on this process, and the key to this process is collecting as specific information as possible and noting significant patterns of strengths and challenges. The equation reads: More specific information collected equals better quality of instruction equals more student learning. For this reason, you are encouraged to gather as much information on students as possible from as many sources as possible. It is crucial to combine your observations with multiple measures of assessment because, as yet, we simply do not have the degree of precision in tests that we would like to believe that we have. Pause and Reflect Self-Monitoring Activity 9.2 is a teacher interview that explores the diagnostic process of the students in your classroom.

Self-Monitoring FYI: Teacher-Made Tests

Points to consider in the development of teacher-made tests:

1. Check to make sure your test questions reflect the content and instructional goals of your content area
2. Try to match your instructional goals with the most appropriate types of items (e.g., essay or objective)
3. Make sure your instructional emphases are reflected in the number of test items
4. Use a variety of objective questions in addition to multiple-choice (e.g., matching, completing, true-false, short answer, rank order, master list)
5. Make sure the directions for the test are clear
6. Use the same language in writing test items as you used in class describing specific content
7. Make sure the test questions are written on an appropriate level of difficulty
8. After scoring the test, evaluate your students' responses:
   - Ask yourself if the questions were too easy or too difficult
   - Notice if there was an item or two that every student missed
   - Ask your students if the test questions were fair and understandable
   - Make adjustments to improve your next test
   - Use test results to adjust future instruction

Self-Monitoring FYI: Standardized Test Reporting

1. Standardized tests are norm-references; as such, the scores reported compare a student's performance with that of a representative group of students (norm group). The raw score on a test is the number of items answered correctly. Raw scores are then converted into norm-referenced scores. Scores are reported for each subtest, and a total achievement score is given.
2. Grade-equivalent scores are expressed in grades and tenths of grades. This score indicates the grade level obtained by the average student in a norm group for a particular number of correct test items. For example, a grade equivalent of 5.8 means the student performed as well as the average student in the eighth month of the fifth grade in the norm group.

Pause and Reflect: Self-Monitoring Activity 9.2

Teacher Interview

To gain an appreciation and a more thorough understanding of the diagnostic process at your grade level, use the following questions to interview your cooperating teacher. Record your respondent's answers and later reflect on them in your journal.

Interview Questions

1. Do you use diagnostic and achievement tests?   Yes   No
   Which ones?

2. Are informal tests used?   Yes   No
   What types?

3. Do you use authentic assessments?   Yes   No
   What types?

4. How do you conduct teacher observations?

Continued

Reflection Questions

1. What is the range of achievement in your class?

2. What are the overall strengths and challenges of your students?

3. How does this affect your instruction?

4. What modifications do you make? Why?

5. Which students are in need of special assistance or instruction?

6. What could you do to assist the special needs of your students?

3. Percentile scores are relative to the percentage of other students falling at or below that score. For example, a percentile rank of 55 means the student performed as well as or better than 55 percent of the norm population.

4. Stanine scores are a type of standard score with a mean of 5 and a standard deviation of approximately 2. Stanines are scores that are distributed into nine parts and range from 1 through 9. Each stanine can be equated to an approximate percentage of scores in the norm group. Stanine 5 is the mean or average score.

Pause and Reflect Self-Monitoring Activity 9.3 (p. 155) provides an examination of how standardized tests are used in your school setting.

Self-Monitoring FYI: Implementing Appropriate Assessment

Following are several suggestions for teachers on appropriate assessment usage in the classroom.

1. Do not be a slave to test scores; be a decision-maker
   - Align instruction with authentic tasks
   - Use multiple measures of assessment
   - Make assessment and diagnosis an ongoing practice
2. Maintain a healthy attitude regarding appropriate information derived from standardized tests
   - Recognize their limitations of time, authenticity, and context
   - Recognize the inherent bias for culturally diverse students
   - Utilize beneficial information that determines what students can do and the strengths they may exhibit
3. Question the categories and labels placed on students by information from standardized tests
   - Do not lower expectations solely on test scores
   - Do not dismiss or perceive students as incapable of learning
   - Seek ways to actively engage the student in learning
4. Establish a climate that values informal measures of assessment
   - Utilize authentic assessment such as portfolios
   - Develop a system of informal observation
   - Develop effective teacher-made tests
   - Involve students in the assessment process

Thinking Like a Teacher: Recap of Major Ideas

- If teachers at any grade level are going to help students become thoughtful, critical, responsive, and effective as learners, the decisions teachers make about instruction need to be made on diagnostic information.

- For assessment to be effective and feasible, we need descriptions and perspectives; we need to know what the assessments look like, how they are constructed and used and their intended purposes.

- Effective teachers collect relevant information on students, interpret and synthesize this information, and instruct according to student needs; they continually evaluate and reshape teaching decisions depending on a student's progress.

- Being able to justify why you are doing what you are doing is one characteristic of an effective teacher.

- The crucial components of monitoring student progress and providing feedback in the direct instruction model are based on the teacher's ability to accurately diagnose and respond to student progress.

- Classroom teachers are expected to diagnose their class at an analytical level at the beginning of the school year and to diagnose students' progress continuously throughout the school year.

- Standardized achievement tests are used with the rationale that these tests interpret an individual's knowledge of content information on the basis of the performance of other students of the same age (norm group) on the same test.

- The purpose of criterion-referenced tests is to assess which student objectives have been achieved in a specific subject.

- Some standardized tests furnish information on students' performance by breaking down a subject area into component parts and providing separate subscores on each component in addition to an overall score.

- Assessment that encompasses students' past, present, and future literacy development is an important concern for classroom teachers.

- Many times teachers and students feel they are passive recipients and targets of assessment rather than active participants and partners in the process when tests are used as measures of accountability.

- Authentic assessments use the active engagement of teachers and students in the assessment process while acknowledging the different needs of policymakers, the community, school personnel, and students.

- Portfolios are collections of authentic tasks gathered across time and across contexts.

- Best pieces portfolio contain examples of work that the student considers to be his or her best efforts.

- Descriptive portfolios enable teachers to gather a wide variety of measures on the children they teach.

- Process portfolios are an intrinsic part of the writing process.

- Accountability portfolios provide part of the basis to determine the quality of instruction for learners in a classroom setting.

Pause and Reflect: Self-Monitoring Activity 9.3

Journal Entry: Standardized Tests

Millions of standardized tests are administered each year to students in schools across the country. How are the results of standardized tests used in your current situation? What decisions are made based on these tests? How do these decisions affect diverse groups of students?

Teacher observation is a powerful diagnostic assessment tool. What are the specific student performance areas you would closely watch in your content area? (If you are in an elementary grade, pick one subject.)

- Sociocultural factors that may cause bias in test results include language or dialect differences, test content, motivation, and attitudes toward the testing situation.

- Culturally different children have not fared well under the "melting pot" theory of education, which emphasizes deficits rather than recognizing differences.

- Informal assessment measures include teacher-made tests, various checklists for particular behaviors, skill inventories, interest inventories, and daily assignments.

- Advantages of teacher-made diagnostic tests over standardized tests include the ability to note more specific strengths and challenges, to more readily establish groups from information collected, and to more closely measure small increments of growth.

- Knowing what to look for and what to listen for and then translating this information into instructional decisions will enable you to better match your teaching techniques to student needs.

Chapter TEN

Teacher Expectations

Teacher expectations are defined as inferences that teachers make about present and future academic achievement and general classroom behavior of students (Good & Brophy, 1986). Expectations for individual students may be based on student record information or on initial contact with students in the classroom. Research on effective schools and teachers has concluded that students learn more if their teachers hold high academic expectations for them (Conforti, 1992; DuPuis & Badialdi, 1987–88; Goodlad, 1984; McDonald & Elias, 1976; Rosenthal & Jacobson, 1968). An experiment conducted by Rosenthal and Jacobson (1968) presented data to suggest that teachers' experimentally induced expectations for student performance were related to actual levels of student performance. Students who were expected to do better even though there was no real basis for this expectation did do better. Thus, teacher expectations are thought to be powerful indicators of student learning.

Critical to the findings of this study is the conclusion that your expectations for students in a learning situation may influence your actions and subsequent learning. Since teachers do form and hold expectations for student behavior and academic achievements, students may sense what is expected of them and behave accordingly. A teacher's expectations may thus become a self-fulfilling prophecy, and classroom teachers might inadvertently undermine the efforts of low-achieving students. Recent studies continue to affirm the importance of teacher expectations and, more importantly, have provided details of how expectations are communicated into actions in the classroom (Avery & Walker, 1993; Fine, 1987; Gay, 1993). These students may essentially receive inferior instruction with less support and encouragement from the teacher.

In a summary of studies, Good and Brophy (1984) ascertained some possible behaviors when teachers communicate low, self-defeating expectations to students:

- Teachers have been observed to provide more time for high-achieving students to respond than for low-achieving students.
- Teachers have been found to respond to incorrect answers of low-achieving students by giving them the answer or calling on another student to answer the question instead of trying to elicit the answers from them.
- Teachers have inappropriately praised marginal or inaccurate student responses, which only emphasizes the academic weakness of such students.
- Teachers have been found to criticize low-achieving students proportionately more frequently than high-achieving students when they provide wrong answers, which is likely to reduce the risk-taking behavior and general initiative of low-achieving students.
- Teachers are less likely to praise low-achieving than high-achieving students when they do provide correct answers even though they may provide fewer correct responses.

- Teachers respond to answers of low-achieving students, especially correct answers, by calling on another student to respond, which results in a failure to confirm the answers.
- Teachers attend more closely to high-achieving students than low-achieving students in the form of smiling more often and maintaining greater eye contact.
- Teachers call on high-achieving students more frequently than low-achieving students.
- Teachers' contact patterns with low-achieving students appear to be different in elementary and secondary classrooms. (High-achieving students dominate public response in elementary classrooms and even more domination occurs in secondary classrooms).
- Teachers demand less from low-achieving students by giving these students easier tests or not asking the students to do genuine academic work (pp. 491–492).

Research has also found that many teachers interact with, call on, praise, and intellectually challenge students who are white, male, and middle-class more than other students in the same classroom and that they reprimand African American male students the most (Jackson & Cosca, 1974; Jones, 1991; Sadker & Sadker, 1982). Teachers are usually unaware that they are showing favoritism, but such bias may benefit members of perceived advantaged social groups when it occurs.

A key word used in the previous discussion was "may." Conversely, a teacher's expectations may *not* have negative effects on some groups of students or individual students. Some students are not as susceptible to teachers' expectations as others. In addition, self-fulfilling prophecies may occur with or without the teacher's awareness that their behavior is being systematically influenced by their attitudes.

Although it is important to hold high expectations for each of your students, it is acceptable to hold differing expectations for various students as long as such expectations are not lowered based on gender, race/ethnicity, socioeconomic status, past school performance, personal characteristics, or other ascribed traits. Relative to these issues, your expectations must not be set in stone but flexible and capable of change based on authentic student performance and ongoing informal/formal assessments. Relevant information accurately collected and recorded may assist you in forming more realistic expectations. Willis (1970) illustrates in her study that the formation of expectations is normal and is inherently neither good nor bad. The critical issue is the accuracy of the expectations and the flexibility with which they are held. Inaccurate expectations will do damage if teachers are unwilling to reexamine them and if instructional decisions are based on them. This Pause and Reflect Self-Monitoring Activity 10.1 will offer you some insight into the interaction patterns that you display to your students.

Pause and Reflect: Self-Monitoring Activity 10.1

Teacher Expectations and Review of Classroom Interaction Patterns

It may surprise you to discover that certain students are rarely involved in classroom happenings. The purpose of this assignment is to make you more aware of the interaction or patterns of teacher-student communication in your class. Ask one of your peers or your cooperating teacher to complete this form while observing you teach two or three lessons. Afterward, reflect on the information by answering the summary questions.

    Directions: Using the seating chart, place a check (✓) in a student's block if a question is directed at the student and a plus sign (+) if the student volunteers or initiates a positive response. Complete this assignment during one direct instruction lesson or class discussion period during the day. If possible, complete for two or three consecutive days during the same period or time period.

Seating chart (may be duplicated for multiple observations)

Continued

Summary Questions

1. Which students were asked more questions? Why?

2. Were there particular groups of students sitting together that received more attention? Why?

3. Which students volunteered readily in class discussions?

4. Which students did not respond in class? Why do you think they did not respond?

5. Did your expectations guide your interactions with students? Why do you think this?

Teacher Efficacy Practices

Effective teachers not only hold and communicate high expectations for their students but also have a strong sense of efficacy ("the individual's perceived expectancy of obtaining academic expectations through personal effort" [Fuller et al., 1982]). In effect, teachers with a high sense of efficacy possess a high degree of professional self-esteem and say, "I know I can teach these students!" Studies have shown a positive relationship between a teacher's sense of efficacy and student achievement (Ashton & Webb, 1986; Ladson-Billings, 1990; 1995). Teachers with a strong sense of efficacy believe teaching makes a difference in student learning, believe in their professional abilities, and believe that putting a high degree of effort into their work will result in higher student achievement.

Teachers with this high sense of efficacy know their subject matter well, like and respect their students, assume personal responsibility for the progress of their students, and believe in their ability to provide culturally responsive instruction to meet the varied needs of all their students. In addition, previous life experiences of teachers—their backgrounds, identities, cultures, and the critical incidents in their lives—help shape their view of teaching as well as essential elements of their practice (Goodson, 1988).

To become a high-efficacy teacher, one overriding requirement is a high degree of effort or commitment. Implementing culturally responsive instruction undoubtedly requires a great deal of awareness, knowledge, and effort, but teachers must have a high degree of commitment to the teaching profession to implement this effectively. These teachers are motivated to put forth extra effort in teaching because they are motivated by pleasing results, not pleasing methods or techniques. Furthermore, high-efficacy teachers take the time and expend the effort to utilize culturally responsive instruction in their classes, not necessarily because they like to incorporate the intensity of teaching students rather than content, but because they are seeking satisfying results from their labors.

Tracking and Ability-Grouping Practices

In *Brown v. Board of Education of Topeka, Kansas* (1954), it was unanimously recognized that segregation of school children, even if the facilities and other tangibles were equal, deprives them of equal (equitable) educational opportunity. However, while *Brown* helped remove legally sanctioned barriers to educational equality, subsequent policies allowing academic tracking and ability grouping drew new boundaries for diverse groups of students as they sought to realize their full potential in school and life. Indeed, few educational issues evoke as much debate and concern as the use of academic tracking and ability grouping (Harris, Ford, Brown, & Carter, 1990) and the continued practice of assigning students to classes based on assessments of academic ability (Adler, 1982; Goodlad, 1984; Slavin & Braddock, 1993).

Generally, ability grouping is associated with elementary schools, and academic tracking is viewed as an artifact of the high school experience. Academic tracking refers to the practice of grouping students according to their performance on standardized tests that are presumed to measure intelligence. Another form of academic tracking involves student self-selection into college preparatory, vocational, or general programs of study. As Ravitch (1985) concludes, academic tracking tends to reflect a student's apparent educational or occupational destiny. By comparison, ability grouping involves placing students into classes or learning groups according to some measure of ability. Kulik (1992) defines it as the homogeneous grouping of same-grade students into groups with varying scholastic aptitude, as determined by testing and other school records.

Meier, Steward, and England (1989) list both academic tracking and ability grouping under the general category of "sorting practices" that take place once students enter school. Oakes (1985) reports that although many people assume that ability grouping and tracking are best for most students, the evidence points clearly to the conclusion that "no group of students has been found to benefit consistently from being in a homogeneous group," and those in the middle and lower groups are often affected negatively (p. 7). In fact, educational activities taking place under the guise of academic tracking and ability grouping impart severe limitations on the potential of many capable students who experience early frustration, resignation to inferior curricula, and low teacher expectations (Wheelock & Hawley, 1992). Too often, these practices account for culturally, linguistically, and economically diverse students dropping out of school (Gill, 1991; Kunjufu, 1989, 1993; Tribble, 1992).

Over the years, opinions on academic tracking and ability grouping have been divided between their supporters and their many detractors. Tracking and ability grouping involve a variety of policy and placement procedures. While most primary schools rely upon within-class grouping, some offer pull-out sections for the gifted or the learning disabled. Some middle schools classify students by ability so that their entire schedule of classes can be determined; others sort students according to subject matter. Additionally, some high schools have only two tracks (regular and college preparatory), while others have several (basic, average, enriched, honors, advanced placement, etc.). The lack of homogeneity in what constitutes tracking explains the confusion and polarities in the literature. Even though researchers recognize many forms of tracking, they persist in lumping schools into categories in order to compare and contrast them (Donelan, Neal, & Jones, 1994).

If your school uses a mixed-ability or heterogeneous setting but offers few core courses, you might consider whether students enjoy sufficient opportunities to learn. Differences also exist in the climate of upper- and lower-track classrooms. On the academic track, higher teacher expectations infuse the classroom climate, students and teachers spend more time on task, teachers spend less time handling discipline, and students and teachers place greater emphasis on learning (Crosby & Owens, 1993). As Oakes (1992) states, the fundamental goal of equalizing opportunity is not simply to mix students with differing abilities, but to increase the quality of instruction for all students attending schools.

To advocate untracking for all students, however, and remain unprepared to work from totally new paradigms is to ignore the magnitude of change that is needed to encourage learning for all students. Thus, teachers and administrators at all levels or experiences must approach academic tracking and ability grouping as major policy issues. There are political issues and operational circumstances residing at the core of tracks: inequitable human and financial resources, inferior facilities and materials, and an overemphasis on discipline and punishment (Braddock & Dawkins, 1993; Richardson & Evans, 1992; Wheelock & Hawley, 1992). With these factors lumped at the core of their education, it is no wonder that students on the lower tracks tend to observe, as Bane (1992) relates, "This place hurts my spirit" (p. 11).

Teachers (and student teachers) of culturally responsive instruction need to hear these voices. The spirit of any public school child is a potentially valuable resource. Academic tracking and ability grouping can devalue and damage the spirits of African American, Hispanic American, Native American, and students of lower socioeconomic status; but society suffers the overall impact. This insidious cycle of low teacher expectations and students who perform at lower levels than they are capable of amounts to a self-fulfilling prophecy, too. Caring educators and parents cannot continue to ignore the stigma attached to children in the lower tracks and the emotional and social affective pain that tracking generates. You must focus instead on equitable opportunity, on how to challenge and encourage students, and on high expectations for all. Effective and culturally responsive instruction encourages higher-order thinking skills and authentic problem-solving, which involve:

- The efficient use of technology
- The best possible use of cooperative working groups
- The creation of learning environments that allow all students to share their experiences
- A willingness to accept students as they are and promote learning from that point forward
- Paying greater attention to the relationship of learning and teaching styles
- A commitment to recruit teachers and administrators of diverse backgrounds
- A reassessment and reorganization of the total curriculum to address vital issues for diverse groups of learners

Finally, you must welcome the knowledge and guidance you may need to structure learning experiences for students that are culturally, linguistically, and economically diverse, even if doing so means that you must confront your own biases. You will do well to be prepared to effectively organize and facilitate stimulating experiences for all students. By seeking to see all students as capable and expect their active involvement, you begin to provide the best in a system of education for all learners.

Other Patterns of "Business as Usual" Affecting Diverse Populations

Additional patterns in schools tend to exhibit and reproduce prevailing race/ethnicity, social class, and gender patterns. Viewing school systems from top to bottom, you may find the following staffing patterns: superintendents are overwhelmingly white and male (95 percent); 27 percent of the principals in the country are women, and though they make up 34 percent of the elementary school principals, they only account for 12 percent of the secondary school principalships (American Association of School Administrators, 1989). Therefore, women and men of color in school administration tend to be elementary school principals, central office staff, or administrators charged with duties related to Title IX, desegregation, etc. Over 90 percent of teachers are white (and the percentage is increasing), with 80 percent of elementary school teachers being female. Mathematics, science, and industrial arts teachers are predominantly male, whereas foreign language, English, and home economics teachers tend to be female. People of color are often custodians, cooks, and aides, while over 90 percent of secretaries in schools are women. These patterns offer distinct role models and authority relationships for students that set up varying levels of expectations. In fact, the preponderance of women at the elementary school level makes it difficult for many boys to identify with school and its requirements. Such patterns make it quite possible that the gap between teachers and students, and especially low socioeconomic-status students and students of color, will widen to become a chasm in many schools.

Summary of Effective Practices

The study of teaching has made tremendous advancements in specifying how effective teachers teach. Goodlad's (1984) study of thirty-eight schools nationwide provides a comprehensive view of what teachers today are teaching. The main finding was school-to-school uniformity, especially at the secondary level. Goodlad also found heavy emphasis on rote learning. Although teachers often said they were developing higher-level thinking skills, their tests overwhelmingly emphasized the regurgitation of memorized material. While many studies have found strong similarities in how teachers teach (Cuban, 1984; Everhart, 1983; Grant & Sleeter, 1986; Sleeter, 1992;), our growing understanding of the teaching process has brought about a greater appreciation of its subtleties and complexities. Providing the appropriate balance of instructional objectives, motivating students, presenting new material correctly to students, providing proper teacher-student interaction and feedback, and maintaining an adequate level of classroom control are but a few of the major areas demanding a teacher's time, expertise, and judgment. In addition, these teaching functions must be performed given the physical characteristics and limitations of the classroom environment and the wide range of individual differences found among any group of students.

Good teaching demands a thorough knowledge of the subject matter. Furthermore, it is important for you to not only use culturally pluralistic and nonsexist materials, but refer often to people of color or women when teaching (Grant & Sleeter, 1986). Second, you should know your students, their developmental characteristics, motivational needs, interests, learning styles, cultural influences, and academic strengths or challenges. Goodlad's (1984) study findings also support the idea that student interest rarely affected what teachers taught. Teachers beefed up or watered down content in response to student skill level. Additionally, it is helpful to remember that student learning is affected by a host of factors ranging from emotional, physical, social, psychological, and neurological factors to out-of-school conditions.

While it is important to know this information about your students, it is equally important to realize that your influence over these factors is minimal. Thus, the principles of instruction serve as a foundation to guide your decision-making. They are attributes that need to be adapted to your particular teaching style, the styles of your students, and the content taught. But, unlike the previous factors over which you have minimal influence, you have direct control over how you choose to interact with and support the learning of your students. Without a professional attitude, however, all knowledge, skills, and strategies will be ineffective (see Figure 10.1).

Teacher commitment to the task of helping all students master important learning objectives is a key consideration differentiating between more- and less-effective teaching. For example, case studies conducted by Brookover et al. (1979) found that schools achieving this prediction were differentially characterized by "teachers' acceptance of responsibility for student achievement" (p. 118), and that this attitude was manifested in a variety of actions involving unusual commitment of their time and energy to help students succeed. Similar conclusions, though using slightly different terminology, have been reached by Bullard and Taylor (1993), Lezotte (1991), Sizemore et al. (1983), and Taylor (1984).

Related to the area of professional commitment is the teacher's attitude of problem-solving. This attitude can be summarized with the statement, "If what we are doing is not working for students, particularly low achievers, we will identify the obstacles we face and try something else that may overcome them" (Banks & Banks, 1995). A teacher's genuine willingness to modify current practices and other approaches epitomizes effective practice and indicates an applied knowledge of the need for culturally responsive pedagogy. The fact that no simple recipe is available for culturally responsive instruction in all situations with all students is exactly what makes teaching so exciting, challenging, and gratifying. For a variety of reasons, multicultural aspects of curriculum and instruction constitute an important consideration

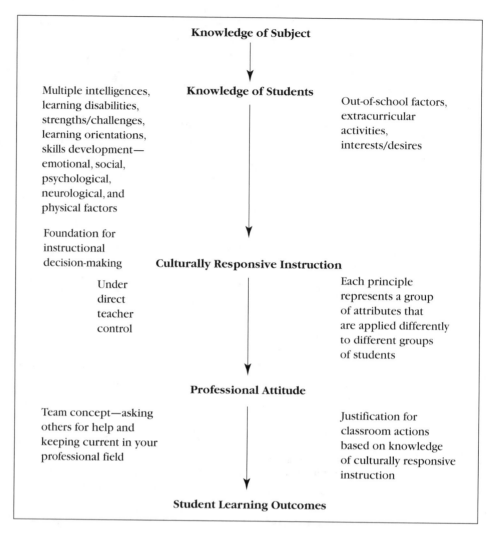

Knowledge of Subject

Knowledge of Students

Multiple intelligences, learning disabilities, strengths/challenges, learning orientations, skills development— emotional, social, psychological, neurological, and physical factors

Out-of-school factors, extracurricular activities, interests/desires

Foundation for instructional decision-making

Culturally Responsive Instruction

Under direct teacher control

Each principle represents a group of attributes that are applied differently to different groups of students

Professional Attitude

Team concept—asking others for help and keeping current in your professional field

Justification for classroom actions based on knowledge of culturally responsive instruction

Student Learning Outcomes

FIGURE 10.1   Key Areas in Teaching–Learning Processes for Culturally Responsive Pedagogy

in striving to improve the achievement of diverse groups of students. Teachers need to continually reflect and make decisions about their programs as they monitor their instructional effectiveness. The principles of instruction presented in this text should be tried in your classrooms and then tested, evaluated, and modified according to your situation.

Teachers committed to focusing on academic improvement for all students tend to exemplify greater cohesiveness and consensus regarding goals than do faculty at less-effective schools. This attitude is first characterized by the admission that you cannot solve all problems in the classroom by yourself. A true professional realizes that he or she is a member of a team within the school community and stays abreast of new knowledge and techniques by participating in professional organizations. High cohesiveness also implies group consensus and cooperation. Many analysts have concluded that "collegiality" is important in improving cohesion and communications, identifying and solving problems, and bolstering other aspects of effectiveness (Rossmiller et al., 1995; Taylor, 1984).

Most importantly, a professional attitude of effectiveness is characterized by justifying your educational decisions not solely on personal opinion but on principles derived from knowing that what you do in the classroom will have a profound effect on students' lives. Go ahead and do what you think best in your situation, but continue to learn and revise your thinking. Also, remember that operating classrooms according to the principle that all children can learn is a central component in respecting and recognizing differences in their cultures and environments.

Pause and Reflect Self-Monitoring Activity 10.2 (pp. 171–72) is an action research project designed to help you explore teacher expectations for diverse classrooms.

In conclusion, a key corollary to the improved opportunities for all students rests in professionalized teaching, which is developed through increasing the knowledge base for teaching and mastery of this knowledge by all teachers permitted to practice. This means providing *all* teachers with a stronger understanding of how children learn and develop, how a variety of curricular and instructional strategies can address student needs, and how changes in school and classroom organization can support student growth and achievement. The students who have, in general, the poorest opportunities to learn are the students who will benefit most from measures that raise the standards of practice for all teachers. As Grant (1989) said: "Teachers who perform high-quality work in urban schools know that, despite reform efforts and endless debates, it is meaningful curricula, dedicated and knowledgeable teachers that make the difference in the education of urban students" (p. 770). When it comes to equalizing opportunities for students to learn, that is the bottom line.

Self-Monitoring FYI: Exploring Your Expectations

1. Consider how your prior experiences inside and outside school are transformed into your classroom strategies. Identify which of these experiences (positive or negative) may have influenced your teaching beliefs or style.

2. Consider the nature of your beliefs about teaching in contemporary schools, especially about your professional commitment to help all children learn.

3. Consider biases or stereotypes you might have for student groups and how these may interfere with your ability to teach some students.

4. Consider how society and all of its schools have become more global, incorporating the values, habits, languages, and customs of various cultures.

5. Consider the fiscal inequities that might exist in schools (e.g., less advantaged schools' problems with supplies, technology, equipment, buses for field trips, small room sizes with large classes, special programs) and plan for how you will address these in some way during your career.

6. Consider the fact that no single method, activity, strategy, or style of teaching is sufficient to adequately teach diverse student populations.

7. Consider how and why you might interact with some students more often and more positively than other students.

8. Consider the many challenges you have in your classroom, in addition to the challenge of teaching academic content effectively.

9. Consider the personal perspectives of your students and how these perspectives, framed by cultural values, provide your students with varied vantage points for learning the content you teach.

10. Consider the nature in which content is transmitted to students and how a sense of professional efficacy is needed.

Thinking Like a Teacher: Recap of Major ideas

- Research on effective schools and teachers has concluded that students learn more if their teachers hold high academic expectations for them.

- Although it is important to hold high expectations for each of your students, it is acceptable to hold differing expectations for various students as long as such expectations are not lowered based on gender, race/ethnicity, socioeconomic status, past school performance, personal characteristics, or other ascribed traits.

- Effective teachers not only hold and communicate high expectations for their students but also have a strong sense of efficacy.

- Teachers with this high sense of efficacy know their subject matter well, like and respect their students, assume personal responsibility for the progress of their students, believe in their ability to provide culturally responsive instruction, and take the time and expend the effort to meet the varied needs of all their students.

- While *Brown* helped remove legally sanctioned barriers to educational equality, subsequent policies allowing academic tracking and ability grouping drew new boundaries of inequity for diverse groups of students.

- Although many people assume that ability grouping and tracking are best for most students, the evidence points clearly to the conclusion that "no group of students has been found to benefit consistently from being in a homogeneous group," and those in the middle and lower groups are often affected negatively.

- Too often, ability grouping and tracking practices account for culturally, linguistically, and economically diverse students dropping out of school.

- Schools tend to exhibit and reproduce prevailing race/ethnicity, social class, and gender patterns with their ability-grouping and tracking procedures.

Pause and Reflect: Self-Monitoring Activity 10.2

Researching Teacher Expectations for Culturally Diverse Classrooms

1. Conduct a teacher-researcher project using teacher interviews and classroom observations to discover teacher expectations for students who are culturally, linguistically, or economically diverse.

2. Explore how experienced teachers develop appropriate expectations for meeting the needs of all their students. Examine their explanations for examples of different kinds of expectations when teaching in schools that have differing populations of students.

3. Record your insights from the interviews and observations.

4. Develop a formal essay that presents your findings, what you have learned, and what more you would like to know about teacher expectations and the success of diverse students.

The following guidelines will provide some criteria that you may use to guide your project and later development of your essay:

1. Locate experienced teachers who are willing to be a part of this project by participating in interviews and observations.

2. If possible, utilize two sites and teachers at differing grade levels.

Continued

3. Explore the teachers' perceptions and theoretical beliefs about education that is multicultural.

4. Inquire about formal and informal experiences that may have contributed to their awareness and knowledge base for teaching different students.

5. As you observe the teachers, look for indications of the teachers' ability to affectively engage students on a personal, social, and academic level.

6. As you observe the teachers, correlate patterns of similarities and differences in instructional styles.

References

Adler, M. J. (1982). *The paideia proposal: An educational manifesto.* New York: Macmillan.

Allington, R. L. (1991). Children who find learning to read difficult: School responses to diversity. In E. H. Hiebert (Ed.), *Literacy for a diverse society: Perspectives, practices, and policies* (pp. 237–252). New York: Teachers College Press.

Alvermann, D. E., Weaver, D., Hinchman, K. A., Moore, D. W., Phelps, S. F., Trash, E. C., & Zalewski, P. (1996). Middle- and high-school students' perceptions of how they experience text-based discussions: A multicase study. Athens, GA: National Reading Research Center. In J. N. Kennedy (Ed.), *R&D Watch* (p. 5). Washington, DC: Council for Educational Development and Research.

American Association of School Administrators. (1989). Personal communication.

Ashton P. T., & Webb, R. B. (1986). *Making a difference: Teachers' sense of efficacy and student achievement.* White Plains, NY: Longman.

Au, K. H. (1993). *Literacy instruction in multicultural settings.* Fort Worth, TX: Harcourt Brace Jovanovich.

Avery, P. G., & Walker, C. (1993). Prospective teachers' perceptions of ethnic and gender differences in academic achievement. *Journal of Teacher Education, 44*(1), 27–37.

Bane, M. W. (Ed.). (1992). *Voices from the inside: A report on schooling from inside the classroom.* Claremont, CA: Graduate school, The Institute for Education in Transformation.

Banks, J. A. (1994). *Multiethnic education theory and practice* (3rd ed.). Boston: Allyn & Bacon.

_____ (1991). *Teaching strategies for ethnic studies* (5th ed.). Boston: Allyn & Bacon.

_____ (1988). *Multiethnic education: Theory and practice* (2nd ed.). Boston: Allyn & Bacon.

_____ (Ed.). (1981). *Education in the 80s: Multiethnic education.* Washington, DC: National Education Association.

Banks, J. A., & Banks, C. A. (1995). *Handbook of research on multicultural education.* New York: Macmillan.

Beane, J. A., & Lipka, R. P. (1986). *Self-concept, self-esteem, and the curriculum.* New York: Teachers College.

Bloom, B. S., Engelhart, M. D., Furst, E. J., Hill, W. H., & Krathwohl, D. R. (Eds.). (1956). *Taxonomy of educational objectives: The classification of education goals, Handbook I: Cognitive domain.* New York: David McKay.

Braddock, J. H., II, & Dawkins, M. P. (1993). Ability grouping, aspirations, and attainments: Evidence from the national education longitudinal study of 1988. *Journal of Negro Education, 62*(3), 324–336.

Brookover, W., Beady, C., Flood, P., Schweitzer, J. & Wisenbaker, J. (1979). *School social systems and student achievement: School can make a difference.* New York: Praeger.

Brophy, J. (1981). Teacher priase: A functional analyses. *Review of Educational Research 51,* 5–32. (ERIC No. EJ 246-420).

Brown v. Board of Education of Topeka, Kansas, 347 U.S. 483. (1954).

Bullard, P., & Taylor, B. O. (1993). *Making school reform happen.* Boston: Allyn & Bacon.

Burns, P. C., Roe, B. D., and Ross, E. P. (1996). *Teaching reading in today's elementary schools.* Boston: Houghton Mifflin.

Buros, O. (Ed.). (1984). *The eighth mental measurement yearbook.* Highland Park, NJ: Gryphon Press.

Cannel, J. J. (1988). Nationally named elementary achievement testing in America's public schools: How all 50 states are above the national average. *Educational Measurement: Issues and Practice, 7*(2), 5–9.

Carlson, S. B. (1985). *Ten designs for assessment and instruction.* Princeton, NJ: Educational Testing Service.

Cazden, C. B. (1988). *Classroom discourse: The language of teaching and learning.* Portsmouth, NH: Heinemann.

Coballes-Vega, C. (1992). *Consideration in teaching culturally diverse children.* Washington, DC: Office of Educational Research and Improvement.

Cohen, E. (1986). *Designing groupwork: Strategies for the heterogeneous classroom.* New York: Teachers College Press.

Cohen, E. (1984). Talking and working together: Status, interaction, and learning. In P. Peterson and L. C. Wilkinson (Eds.), *The social context of instruction: Group organization and processes* (pp. 171–187). New York: Academic Press.

Conforti, J. M. (1992). The legitimation of inequity in American education. *Urban Review, 24*(4), 227–238.

Crosby, M. S., & Owens, E. M. (March, 1993). The disadvantages of tracking and ability grouping: A look at cooperative learning as an alternative. *Solutions and Strategies, 5,* 1–9.

Cuban, L. (1984). *How teachers taught.* New York: Longman.

Cummins, J. (1986). *Empowering minority students: A framework for intervention.* Sacramento, CA: CABE.

Darling-Hammond, L., & Wise, A. E. (1985). Beyond standardization: State standards and school improvement. *Elementary School Journal, 85*(3), 315–336.

DeAvila, E. (1986). *Finding out/descubrimiento.* Northvale, NJ: Santillana Publishing Company.

Delpit, L. (1995). *Other people's children: Cultural conflict in the classroom.* New York: The New Press.

Donelan, R. W., Neal, G. A., & Jones, D. L. (1994). The promise of *Brown* and the reality of academic groping: The tracks of my tears. *The Journal of Negro Education, 63*(3), 376–388.

DuPus, V., & Badialdi, B. (1987–88). Classroom climate and teacher expectations in homogeneously grouped secondary schools. *Journal of Classroom Interaction, 23*(1), 28–33.

Dwyer, C. (1991). Language, culture and writing (working paper 13). Berkeley, CA: Center for the Study of Writing, University of California.

Emmer, E. T., Evertson, C. M., Clements, B. S., & Worsham, M. E. (1997). *Classroom management for secondary teachers* (4th ed.). Boston: Allyn & Bacon.

Everhart, R. (1983). *Reading, writing, and resistance.* Boston: Routledge & Kegan Paul.

Evertson, C. M., Emmer, E. T., Clements, B. S., & Worsham, M. E. (1997). *Classroom management for secondary teachers* (4th ed.). Boston: Allyn & Bacon.

Fine, M. (1987). Silencing in public schools. *Language Arts, 64*(2), 157–174.

Fisher, C., Berliner, D., Filby, N., Marliave, R., Cahen, L., and Dishaw, M. (1980). Teaching behaviors, academic learning time, and student achievement: An overview. In C. Denham and A. Lieberman (Eds.), *Time to learn*. Washington, DC: National Institute of Education.

Fisher, C., Berliner, D. C., Filby, N. N., Marliave, R., Cahen, L. S., Dishaw, M. M., & Moore, J. E. (1978). *Teaching and learning in the elementary school: A summary of the Beginning Teacher Evaluation Study*. Washington, DC: National Institute of Education.

Fordham, S. (1991). Peer-proofing academic competition among Black adolescents: 'Acting White' Black American style. In C. E. Sleeter (Ed.), *Empowerment through multicultural education* (pp. 69–93). Albany: State University of New York Press.

Fuller, B., Wood, K., Rapport, T., & Dornbusch, S. (1982). The organizational content of individual efficacy. *Review of Educational Research, 52,* 7–30.

Fuller, M. L. (1996). Multicultural concerns and classroom management. In C. A. Grant and M. L. Gomez (Eds.), *Making schooling multicultural,* Chapter 7, pp. 133–158. Englewood Cliffs, NJ: Prentice Hall.

Garcia, E. (1992). Effective instruction for language minority students: The teacher. *Journal of Education, 173*(2), 130–141.

Gardner, H. (1983). *Frames of mind*. New York: Basic Books.

Gay, G. (1993). Building cultural bridges: A bold proposal for teacher education. *Education and Urban Society, 25*(3), 285–299.

Gill, W. (1991). *Issues in African-American education*. Nashville, TN: One Horn Press.

Gilmore, P. (1983). Spelling 'Mississippi': Recontextualizing a literacy-related speech event. *Anthropology & Education Quarterly, 14*(4), 75–79.

Golnick, D. M., & Chinn, P. C. (1986). *Multicultural education in a pluralistic society*. New York: Maxwell Macmillian International Press.

Good, T., & Brophy, J. (1986). School effects. In M. Wittrock (Ed.), *Handbook of research on teaching* (3rd ed.). New York: Macmillan.

Good, T., & Brophy, J. (1984). *Looking in classrooms* (3rd ed.), pp. 491–492. New York: Harper & Row.

Goodlad, J. I. (1984). *A place called school*. New York: McGraw–Hill.

Goodman, Y. (1980). The roots of literacy. In M. P. Douglass (Ed.), *Reading: A humanizing experience* (pp. 286–301). Claremont: Claremont Graduate School.

Goodson, I. (1988). Curriculum as structured inequality. Paper presented at the Annual Meeting of the American Educational Research Association, New Orleans, LA.

Grant, C. A. (1989). Urban teachers: Their new colleagues and curriculum. *Phi Delta Kappan, 70*(10), 764–778.

Grant, C. A., & Sleeter, C. E. (1986). *After the school bell rings*. London: Falmer Press.

Graves, D. (1983). *Writing: Teachers and children at work*. Exeter, NH: Heinemann.

Greenfield, E. (1973). *Rosa Parks*. New York: Crowell.

Haney, W., & Madaus, G. (1989). Searching for alternatives to standardized tests: Whys, whats and whithers. *Phi Delta Kappan, 70,* 683–687.

Hansen, J. (1987). *When writers read*. Portsmouth, NH: Heinemann.

Harris, E. L. (1992). A principal and the evolution of a school culture: A case study. *Planning and changing, 23*(1), 29–44.

Harris, J. J., III, Ford, D. Y., Brown, F., & Carter, D. G., Sr. (1990). The effects of ability groups and tests on student vocational counseling and placement. In S. S. Goldberg (Ed.), *Readings on equal education: Critical issues for a new administration* (Vol. 10) (pp. 153–168). New York: AMS.

Harris, T. L., & Hodges, R. E. (1995). *The literacy dictionary: The vocabulary of reading and writing.* Newark, DE: International Reading Association.

Heath, S. B. (1981). Towards an ethnohistory of writing in American education. In M. Farr-Whitman (Ed.), *Variation in writing: Functional and linguistic-cultural differences, Vol. 1 of writing: The nature, development and teaching of written communication* (pp. 225–246). 2 Vols. Hillsdale, NJ: Lawrence Erlbaum.

Hernandez, H. (1990). *Multicultural education: A teacher's guide to content and process.* Columbus, OH: Merrill.

Heilman, A. W., Blair, T. R., & Rupley, W. H. (1998). *Principles and practices of teaching reading* (9th ed.). Upper Saddle River, NJ: Merrill/Prentice Hall.

Jackson, G., & Cosca, C. (1974). The inequality of educational opportunity in the Southwest: An observational study of ethnically mixed classrooms. *American Educational Research Journal, 11,* 219–229.

Jacob, E., & Sanday, P. R. (1976). Dropping out: A strategy for coping with cultural pluralism. In P. R. Sanday (Ed.), *Anthropology and the public interest: Fieldwork and theory* (pp. 95–110). New York: Academic Press.

Jones, D. L. (1991). The relationship of process oriented assessment and minority student participation during a reading lesson. Unpublished doctoral dissertation, College Station, TX: Texas A & M University.

Johnson, D. W. (1990). *Reaching out* (4th ed.). Englewood Cliffs, NJ: Prentice Hall.

Johnston, P. (1984). Assessment in reading: The emperor has no clothes. In P. D. Pearson (Ed.), *Handbook of Reading Research* (pp. 147–182). New York: Longman.

Koretz, D. M. (1991). State comparisons using NAEP: Large costs, disappointing benefits. *Educational Researcher, 20*(3), 19–21.

Kounin, J. S. (1970). *Discipline and group management in classrooms.* New York: Holt, Rinehart & Winston.

Kunjufu, J. (1993). *Hip-hip vs. MAAT: A psycho/social analysis of values.* Chicago: African American Images.

Kunjufu, J. (1989). *A talk with Jawanza: Critical issues in educating African American youth.* Chicago: African American Images.

Kuykendall, C. (1992). *From rage to hope: Strategies for reclaiming Black & Hispanic students.* Bloomington, IN: National Educational Service.

Ladson-Billings, G. (1995). But that's just good teaching: The case for culturally relevant pedagogy. *Theory into Practice, 34*(3), 159–165.

Ladson-Billings, G. (1990). Like lightning in a bottle: Attempting to capture the pedagogical excellence of successful teachers of Black students. *International Journal of Qualitative Studies in Education, 3,* 335–344.

Lewis, A. C. (1991). *The kids' guide to social action.* New York: Edna McConnell Clark Fundation.

Lezotte, L. W. (1991). *Correlates of effective schools.* Okemos, MI: Effective School Publications.

Linn, M. C. (1985). Gender equity in computer learning environments. *Computers and the Social Sciences, 1*(1), 19–27.

Linn, R. L., Graue, R. & Sanders, T. (1990). Comparing state and district results to national norms: The validity of the claims that "everyone is above average". *Educational Measurement: Issues and Practice, 9*(3), 5–14.

Louis, Ai-Ling. (1982). *Yeh-Shen: A Cinderella Story from China.* New York: Philomel Books.

Maslow, A. H. (1943). A theory of human motivation. *The Psychological Review, 50,* 370–396.

McCarty, T. L., Lynch, R. H., Wallace, S., & Bennally, A. (1991). Classroom inquiry and Navajo learning styles: A call for reassessment. *Anthropology & Education Quarterly, 22*(1), 42–59.

McDonald, F., & Elias, P. (1976). *Beginning teacher evaluation study, Phase II,* 1973–74. Princeton, NJ: Educational Testing Service.

McLaren, P. (1989). *Life in schools: An introduction to critical pedagogy in the foundations of education.* New York: Longman.

Meier, K. J., Stewart, J., Jr., & England, R. E. (1989). *Race, class, and education: The politics of second-generation discrimination.* Madison, WI: University of Wisconsin Press.

Michaels, S. (1986). Narrative presentations: An oral preparation for literacy. In J. Cook-Gumperz (Ed.), *The social construction of literacy* (pp. 94–116). Cambridge: Cambridge University Press.

_____ (1981). "Sharing time": Children's narrative styles and differential access to literacy. *Language in Society, 10*(3), 423–442.

Miller-Jones, D. (1989). Culture and testing. *American Psychologist, 44,* 360–366.

Morrison, T. (1970). *The Bluest Eye.* New York: Holt, Rinehart and Winston.

Nickerson, R. (1989). New directions in educational assessment. *Educational Researcher, 18,* 3–7.

Oakes, J. (1992). Grouping students for instruction. In M. C. Alkin (Ed.), *Encyclopedia of educational research* (6th ed., Vol. 20) (pp. 562–567). New York: Macmillan.

Oakes, J. (1985). *Keeping track: How schools structure inequality.* New Haven, CT: Yale University Press.

Ogbu, J. U. (1987). Variability in minority school performance: A problem in search of an explanation. *Anthropology & Education Quarterly, 18*(4), 312–334.

Palinscar, A. S., & Brown, A. C. (1984). Reciprocal teaching of comprehension-fostering and comprehension monitoring activities. *Cognition and Instruction 1,* 117– 75.

Pallas, A. M., Natriello, G., & McDill, E. L. (1989). The changing nature of the disadvantaged population: Current dimensions and future trends. *Educational Researcher,* 18, 16–22.

Pappas, C. C., Kiefer, B. Z., & Levstik, L. (1995). *An integrated perspective in the elementary school: Theory into action.* White Plains, NY: Longman.

Parekh, B. (1986). The concept of multicultural education. In S. Modgil, G. K. Verma, K. Mallick, & C. Modgil (Eds.). *Multicultural education: The interminable debate* (pp. 19–31). Philadephia: Falmer Press.

Paulson, F. L., Paulson, P. R., & Meyer, C. A. (1991). What makes a portfolio a portfolio? *Educational Leadership, 49,* 60–63.

Phelan, P., Davidson, A. L., & Cao, H. T. (1991). Students' multiple worlds: Negotiating the boundaries of family, peer, and school cultures. *Anthropology & Education Quarterly, 22*(3), 224–250.

Philips, S. U. (1983). *The invisible culture: Communication in classroom community on the Warms Springs Indian reservation.* New York: Longman.

Purves, A. C., & Beach, R. (1972). Literature and the reader: Research in response to literature, reading interests, and the teaching of literature. Final report to the National Endowment for the Humanities, Washington, DC.

Rasinski, T. V., & Padak, N. D. (1990). Multicultural learning through children's literature. *Language Arts, 67*(6), 576–580.

Raths, J. (1971). Teaching without specific objectives. *Educational Leadership, 28,* 714–720.

Raths, L. E. (1972). *Meeting the needs of children: Creating trust and security.* Columbus, OH: Merrill.

Ravitch, D. (1985). *The schools we deserve.* New York: Basic Books.

Resnick, L., & Resnick, D. (1990). Tests as standards of achievements in school. *The uses of standardized tests in American education* (pp. 63–80). Princeton, NJ: Educational Testing Service.

Richardson, R. C., & Evans, E. T. (1992, June). *African American males: Endangered species and the most paddled.* Paper presented at the Annual Conference of the Louisiana Association of Multicultural Education, Baton Rouge, LA.

Rosenberg, J. (1974). *Eliminating ethnic bias in instructional materials: Comment and bibliography.* Washington, DC: Association for Supervision and Curriculum.

Rosenshine, B., & Stevens, R. (1995). Functions for teaching well-structured tasks. In Rosenshine, B. (Ed.), Advances in research on instruction, *Journal of Educatgional Research,* 88, 262–268.

Rosenshine, B., & Stevens, R. (1986). Teaching functions. In M. C. Wittrock (Ed.), *Handbook of research on teaching.* New York: Macmillan.

Rosenthal, R., & Jacobson, L. (1968). *Pygmalion in the classroom: Teacher expectations and pupils' intellectual development.* New York: Holt, Rinehart & Winston.

Rossmiller, R. A., Holcomb, E. L., & McIsaac, D. N. (1995). *The effective schools process.* Madison, WI: National Center for Effective Schools Research and Development.

Sadker, M., & Sadker, A. (1982). *Sex equity handbook for schools.* New York: Longman.

Schniedewind, N., & Davidson, E. (1983). *Open minds to equality: A sourcebook of learning activities to promote race, sex, class, and age equity.* Boston: Allyn & Bacon.

Shepard, L. (1990). Using assessment to improve learning. *Educational Leadership,* 52(5), 38–43.

Shepard, L. (1989). Why we need better assessments. *Educational Leadership, 47,* 4–9.

Sizemore, B. A., Brossard, C. A., & Harrigan, B. (1983). *An abashing anomaly: The high achieving predominately Black elementary school* (Abstract NIE-G-80-0006). Pittsburg: University of Pittsburgh.

Slavin, R. E. (1997). *Educational psychology: Theory and practice* (5th ed.). Boston: Allyn & Bacon.

Slavin, R. E., & Braddock, J. H., II. (1993, Summer). Ability grouping: On the wrong track. *College Board Review, 168,* 11–18.

Sleeter, C. E. (1992). *Keepers of the American dream.* London: Falmer Press.

Sleeter, C. E., & Grant, C. A. (1993). Five approaches to race, class and gender. *Comparative Education Review, 37* (1), 62–68.

Smith, M. L. (1991). Put to the test: The effects of external testing on teachers. *Educational Researcher, 20*(5), 8–11.

Soar, R. S., & Soar, R. M. (1983). Content effects in the teaching-learning process. In D. C. Smith (Ed.), *Essential knowledge for beginning educators* (65–75). Washington, DC: American Association of Colleges for Teacher Education. (ERIC No. SP 022 600).

Spindler, G., & Spindler, L. (1990). *The American cultural dialogue and its transmission.* London: Falmer Press.

Stallings, J., & Mohlman, G. (1981). *School policy, leadership style, teacher change and student behavior in eight schools,* Final report. Washington, DC: National Institute of Education.

Steptoe, J. (1987). *Mufaro's beautiful daughters: An African tale*. New York: Lothrop, Lee & Shepard Books.

Sternberg, R. J. (1983). Criteria for intellectual skills training. *Educational Researcher, 12*(2), 6–12.

Suhor, C. (1985). Objective tests and writing samples: How do they affect instruction in composition? *Phi Delta Kappan, 66,* 635–639.

Taylor, P. O. (1984). *Implementing what works: Elementary principals and school improvement programs*. Unpublished doctoral dissertation, Northwestern University, Evanston, IL.

Tharp, R. G., & Gillimore, R. (1988). *Rousing minds to life: Teaching, learning and schooling in social context*. Cambridge: Cambridge University Press.

Tribble, I., Jr. (1992). *Making their mark: Educating African-American children*. Silver Spring, MD: Beckham House.

Trueba, H. T. (1988). Peer socialization among minority students: A high school dropout prevention program. In H. Trueba and C. Delgado-Gaitan (Eds.), *Schools and society: Learning content through culture*. New York: Praeger Publishers.

Trueba, H. T., Jacobs, L., & Kirton, E. (1990). *Cultural conflict and adaptation: The case of Hmong children in American society*. London: Falmer Press.

Vacca, R. T., & Vacca, J. L. (1986). *Content area reading* (2nd ed.). Boston: Little, Brown.

Villegas, A. M. (1991). *Culturally responsive pedagogy for the 1990's and beyond*. Princeton, NJ: Educational Testing Service.

Walker, C. L. (1987). Hispanic achievements: Old views and new perspectives. In H. Trueba (Ed.), *Success or failure: Learning and the language minority student* (pp. 15–32). Cambridge, MA: Newbury House.

Walker-Dalhouse, D. (1992). Fostering multi-cultural awareness: Books for young children. *Reading Horizons, 33*(1), 47–54.

Wassermann, S. (1987). Teaching for thinking: Louis E. Raths revisited. *Kappan, 68,* 460–465.

Wheelock, A., & Hawley, W. D. (1992). *Crossing the tracks*. New York: New World Press.

Willis, B. (1970). The influence of teacher expectation on teachers' classroom interaction with selected children. *Dissertation Abstracts, 30,* 5072A.

Winograd, P., & Jones, D. L. (1992). The use of portfolios in performance assessment. *New Directions for Education Reform, 1*(2), 5–12.

Winograd, P., & Paris, S. G. (1988). A cognitive and motivational agenda for reading instruction. *Educational Leadership, 46*(4), 30–36.

Index

Notes

Notes

Notes

Notes

Notes

Notes

Notes

Notes